Individual Rights and Civic Responsibility

THE RIGHT TO FREEDOM FROM SEARCHES

Fred Ramen

The Rosen Publishing Group, Inc.
New York

Published in 2001 by The Rosen Publishing Group, Inc.
29 East 21st Street, New York, NY 10010

First Edition

Library of Congress Cataloging-in-Publication Data

Ramen, Fred
The right to freedom from searches / by Fred Ramen.— 1st ed.
p. cm. — (Individual rights and civic responsibility)
Includes bibliographical references and index.
ISBN 0-8239-3237-0
1. Searches and seizures—United States—Juvenile literature. 2. United States. Constitution. 4th Amendment—Juvenile literature. [1. Searches and seizures. 2. United States. Constitution. 4th Amendment.]
I. Title.II. Series.
KF9630.Z9 R36 2000
345.73'0522—dc21 00-010829

Manufactured in the United States of America

About the Author

Fred Ramen is a writer and computer programmer who lives in New York City. He is also the author of *The Rights of the Accused* and *Influenza* for The Rosen Publishing Group. Fred's interests include the American Civil War, aikido, and the novels of Raymond Chandler. He was a semifinalist in the 1997 *Jeopardy!* Tournament of Champions.

For Jeff Ramen

Contents

Introduction

The United States Constitution has proven to be one of the most important documents in the history of the world. Its brilliant plan of government, which has safely guarded democracy and liberty in this country since its adoption in 1789, has become a beacon of freedom for everyone in the world. Fundamental to the theory behind the U.S. Constitution, and the reason it has so successfully protected the rights of its citizens, is the idea that the powers of government must be limited. By restricting the powers of the government, the Constitution not only protects its citizens but makes a powerful statement on what the role of government in human affairs should be.

Because of this, the first ten amendments to the Constitution—the Bill of Rights—are perhaps even more important than the original document itself. The Bill of Rights consists of a series of guarantees by the government not to do something—whether it is not to restrict the freedom of the press to print stories inconvenient for the government, or not to take land or property from citizens without giving them fair payment. Even more than the original Constitution, these amendments represent the basic promise of fairness and honesty toward all that is central to the American political system.

A government's true nature is best shown in its justice system. Because of this, a great many of the rights protected by the Bill of Rights have to do with the rights of people accused of a crime. The events that led up to the Revolutionary War, when the British abused their own court system in order to persecute Americans opposed to their policies, caused many in the United States to have an intense desire to make sure that their system could never be so abused. The Bill of Rights reflects their concerns by including a series of rules that the government cannot violate when it puts a person on trial for committing a crime, providing a procedure that makes sure that every person receives a fair and impartial trial.

The Fourth, Fifth, Sixth, and Eighth Amendments to the U.S. Constitution all deal with what are known as the "rights of the accused." All offer not only specific protections for people accused of a crime but also impose restrictions on the kinds of actions that the government can take when it accuses someone of a crime. Among these amendments, the Fourth Amendment contains some of the most important and profound limitations on the powers of the government. Created in memory of some of the worst abuses of justice that the British committed against the colonists, the protections of the Fourth Amendment have long been considered the bedrock of American justice. However, like all the protections of the Bill of Rights, it was not until the twentieth century that this amendment finally came to protect all citizens of the United States equally, no matter where they lived.

The Fourth Amendment concerns searches and seizures and warrants. Legally, searches and seizures refers to the ability of the government to search a person or his or her home or office and to seize items that are evidence of a crime that the person may have committed; this evidence then can be used against him or her at trial. The Fourth Amendment requires that searches and seizures must be reasonable. Determining what exactly reasonable means has been the subject of many important Supreme Court decisions about the Fourth Amendment, but a reasonable search usually requires a warrant.

A warrant is a document, usually issued by a judge, that allows the police to search a place or put a person under arrest. In order for the warrant to be issued, the government must demonstrate that it has probable cause to believe that the person covered in the warrant has committed a crime. In general, evidence that has been collected by a search performed without a warrant is not allowed to be used at trial; however, there are certain exceptions to this rule. The history of how this rule came to be part of the trial system, and exactly where those exceptions lie, is another part of the interesting story of the Fourth Amendment.

As new technologies have been created, the Fourth Amendment definition of "persons, houses, papers, and effects" that are protected by it has had to be reinterpreted by the Supreme Court. Questions such as, "Can the police search a car without a warrant?" and "Is wire-tapping illegal?" have provoked some controversial decisions by the Court.

Over the years, the Supreme Court has interpreted the Fourth Amendment and the other protections of the Bill of Rights, and created an intricate, tightly controlled system dedicated to the principle that not only must a person be given every opportunity to prove his or her innocence, but in addition, the government must disprove that innocence beyond any reasonable doubt. This delicate balance between accused and accuser, citizen and government, has frequently become a source of controversy, and it always has been difficult to determine exactly how the balance should be maintained. But for two hundred years, the Bill of Rights, and behind it the U.S. Constitution, has served as a guiding principle for those charged with the enormous duty of protecting the rights of American citizens.

The U.S. Constitution thus provides for an amazing and unprecedented amount of protection from government oppression. Even more impressive, however, is that the Constitution exists at all. When it was written, it was practically the only document of its kind in the world. Nowhere else was it felt necessary to lay out a specific plan of government for a nation—let alone one that limited so severely the powers of the national government. Yet the founders felt the need for such a document, and the one they created has stood the test of time.

Even more important, the Constitution has continued to expand and grow. As time has passed, our interpretations of it have expanded the scope of the protections it grants to U.S. citizens, providing even more liberty than it did when first ratified. This amazing document is a dynamic thing, one that continues to keep pace with the changing face of America.

1 The United States Constitution

During the Revolutionary War, as a part of their amazing experiment with democracy, each of the former colonies created its own state constitution. Accustomed to the British legal system, the colonies wanted to have documents that would put basic limitations on the power of the government over the lives of the citizens of each state. What is interesting, however, is how they improved on the model of the "British Constitution," the largely unwritten body of law and precedent that relies on a few key documents, such as the Magna Carta and the English Bill of Rights. In contrast, the constitutions the states drafted instead provided a complete blueprint for the government of each state.

Each state created a government in which an elected legislature would represent the people. Many states, such as Virginia, also included basic guarantees of the rights of their citizens. These state constitutions and bills of rights would become valuable models for the United States Constitution.

However, although the citizens of each state had created strong plans for their own government, they did not do so for the country as a whole. Under an agreement called the Articles of Confederation, the citizens of the now-independent United States created a national government with almost no real power. Rather than being united under a central government with the authority to override the interests of individual states when they conflicted with the interests of the country, the United States under the Articles of Confederation was essentially a loose collection of individual republics. Representation in Congress was by state, not population, and Congress had authority to rule only on truly national matters, such as whether or not to declare war. The states were left alone in many important matters, such as coining money and taxing products from other states—a situation that made financial matters in the new country extremely confused. Congress lacked the power to tax the states directly; the best it could do was to ask for donations from them. But without an executive branch that was charged with enforcing the laws, there was no way to make the states respect these requests. And because any changes to the Articles required the consent of all the states, it was very difficult to reform them.

This fundamental weakness endangered the very existence of the United States. Had the Articles of Confederation continued as the law of the land, the government could have collapsed, or lost any real power, leaving a collection of puny republics along the eastern coast of North America in its place. Already, financial disputes between the states were threatening the health of the nation. A taxpayers' revolt in Massachusetts had to be put down, with great difficulty, by the local militia—the national government proved powerless to react to the situation. Calls for modification of the Articles began to be heard from all parts of the country; many leading Americans felt that a stronger national government had to be created soon.

In 1787, because of this mounting pressure and criticism, Congress called the Constitutional Convention to meet to revise the Articles. Gathering in Philadelphia, the members of the convention (which included delegations from every state except Rhode Island) soon decided to abandon this limited goal. They began to draft a new document that would substantially change the form of the national government, replacing it with a more centralized and powerful organization.

The convention included many of the leading citizens of America, men with much experience in both local and national government. Eight signers of the Declaration of Independence, including Benjamin Franklin, attended. Thirty-nine members out of the total of fifty-five had served in Congress, and more than thirty were veterans of the Revolutionary War. General George Washington, who had been in quiet retirement in Virginia, attended the convention and was made its president. Chief among the men who actually wrote the Constitution were New York's Alexander Hamilton and Virginia's James Madison; two other men who were highly influential were the Pennsylvanians James Wilson and Gouveneur James Morris, who helped write the famous preamble to the Constitution.

There were three major problems that confronted the convention. First was to find the best way to represent the people in the government—in other words, how to organize the

The Magna Carta

One of the most important documents in English history was the Magna Carta (Latin for "Great Charter") issued by King John to his barons in 1215. This charter was important for several reasons. First, it was not simply granted by the king but was demanded by his subjects. Second, it made many reforms to the justice system to protect the rights of the English and to make the system more fair. Perhaps most important, it set out definite limits to the king's power and warned him that if he violated the charter, the barons had the right to rebel and try to remove him. Although the Magna Carta actually did little to help the common people of England (it was after all written by the nobility to protect themselves from the king), its principles—to limit the power of government and to guarantee certain rights—became the central idea of English law.

The Magna Carta, along with the English Bill of Rights of 1689, were not only the sources of the right to liberty the colonists felt was their due as Englishmen, but also served as models for the U.S. Constitution and the Bill of Rights.

national legislature. Many favored a plan similar to the structure of the existing Congress: Each state would have equal representation in the national government. This would give the smaller states as much power as the bigger states. Others, such as Madison, favored making representation in the new Congress based on the population of the states the members were elected from; this way, the larger states would have more power. Eventually, a compromise was worked out. The Congress would be split into two houses, along the same pattern as the British Parliament, which consists of an "upper" House of Lords, composed only of noblemen, and a "lower" House of Commons, composed of people elected by British citizens. The upper house of Congress would be the Senate, and each state would send two representatives to it. (These senators were originally elected by the legislatures of the states; the Constitution was later amended to make them elected directly by the people of the state.) The lower house would be the House of Representatives. Each state would send a certain number of congressmen to this house based on the population of the state. The founders then created a careful balance of power between the two houses. The Senate was given more power over issues of national or international importance; it confirms the appointment of cabinet members or Supreme Court justices, as well as international treaties. The House, on the other hand, was given control over tax laws and other bills to raise money. Both houses of Congress must approve a bill for it to become law, however.

This careful balance of power is known as checks and balances and runs throughout the Constitution. By dividing power between the three main branches of the government—the legislative branch (Congress), which writes laws;

What Is Federalism?

Federalism is a system whereby the powers of government are divided between national and local governments. A local government gives up some of its powers to the national government in return for guarantees from the national government that it will not interfere in purely local matters.

The basic units of American federalism are the states and the federal government. Under the Constitution, a basic division of powers was set up. The federal government was given authority over matters of national interest or those areas necessary for a stable country—deciding whether or not to go to war, or the creation of a national currency, for example. The Constitution grants only certain very specific powers to the federal government; the states are free to act in all matters not covered by the authority of the federal government. This principle was reinforced by the Tenth Amendment, which states that those powers not specifically given to the federal government or denied the states are reserved for the states or the people.

One reason the founders established a federal republic was that it acted as a system of checks and balances. After the Revolution, many people feared a strong central government, and this new system seemed to guarantee that the national government would not intrude on the lives of ordinary citizens. However, the tensions within the federal system eventually erupted into the Civil War. Since that time, the power of the federal government has gradually increased, as the Fourteenth Amendment and the great crises of the twentieth century—the Great Depression and the two World Wars—have required more and more intervention by the national government into local affairs.

the executive branch (the president and the federal bureaucracy), which enforces laws, and the judicial branch (the Supreme Court and the lower federal courts), which interprets laws—the founders created a system that made it almost impossible for the members of any one branch to take over the powers of another. This was a vital concern for men who had fought a war to end the control of a king over their lives and of crucial importance in addressing their next major challenge: creating a strong executive branch that would be able to enforce the will of Congress.

Many people in the United States, including many at the convention, were against the very idea of having a president. Many republics throughout history had failed because one man had seized power and become a tyrant, sometimes by working through the system, as Adolf Hitler would do in the future in Germany. At the same time, the rudderless structure of the Articles of Confederation made it clear to many that some sort of official who had the power to use the government to enforce its own laws was needed. The compromise that the founders settled on was to have a president who was the head of the government but had very little ability to change the government. Although the president was the commander-in-chief of the United States military, only Congress could declare war. Although the president could veto, or refuse to sign into law, a bill from Congress that he disagreed with, Congress could override this veto if two-thirds of the members of each house voted to do so. In this way, the founders felt that they had created a workable balance between giving the president too little and too much power, although the office remained one of the most controversial parts of their new plan.

The Amendment Process

Realizing that no document that they could produce would be either perfect or able to meet all the challenges of the future, the founders were careful to include an amendment process in the U.S. Constitution that would allow it to be changed if enough people were convinced of the necessity of doing so. Further, they made sure to avoid the mistakes of the Articles of Confederation, which required that all the states approve a change before it could take place.

Article V of the Constitution gives two methods for proposing and approving an amendment. The first is for two-thirds of each house of Congress to approve an amendment and then send it out to the states. If three-quarters of the state legislatures approve the amendment, it becomes a part of the Constitution. The second way is that if two-thirds of the state legislatures call for a convention, they can meet to propose and approve new amendments. As this is practically the same thing as calling a new constitutional convention, it has never happened.

Over the years, thirty-three amendments have been proposed, and twenty-seven ratified. For example, the Twenty-first Amendment repealed the Eighteenth Amendment, which prohibited the manufacture and sale of alcoholic beverages in the United States from 1920 to 1933. (During this time, called the Prohibition era, law enforcement officials destroyed all alcoholic beverages, as shown in the photograph above.) The most important amendments covered in this book are the first ten (collectively called the Bill of Rights) and the Fourteenth Amendment, which expanded their protections greatly in the years following the Civil War.

The final issue the founders had to deal with was how to bring some stability to the American financial situation. This in many ways proved to be the easiest matter of all to resolve. Congress was given the power to directly tax the nation, and the president was given the power to enforce these laws. (In fact, President Washington would later use the powers of the federal government to put down a tax rebellion in Pennsylvania in an early test of the new Constitution.) Only the federal government (not the states) had the right to coin money, and Congress was given the power to regulate any trade between states, preventing the trade wars between rival states that had cropped up under the Articles.

The final piece of the constitutional puzzle was the creation of the Supreme Court. Originally, it possessed little power; it had the right to decide cases between different states, or between the U.S. government and state governments. In time, however, the Supreme Court would assert a power that made it the equal of the other branches in terms of how it could affect the laws of the nation: the ability to decide whether or not a law violated the U.S. Constitution and the power to strike down any law that failed that test.

The new Constitution was superior in almost every respect to the Articles of Confederation. But now it had to face an important test: ratification, the agreement by the individual states to accept it as the new supreme law of the land. Out of the fiery debate over this crucial issue of the nation's early history came a new, striking addition to the Constitution, a collection of rules that would soon be regarded as a shining beacon of liberty: the Bill of Rights.

2 The Birth of the Bill of Rights

The debate over the ratification of the Constitution was hard-fought on both sides. Two opposing parties emerged: the Federalists, led by Alexander Hamilton and James Madison, who supported the new Constitution, and the Antifederalists, who opposed the Constitution. In a brilliant series of essays, later collected as the *Federalist Papers*, Hamilton and Madison defended the Federalist cause and helped calm the fears of those who opposed the idea of a strong central government. Still, the new plan was closely contested throughout the country, and the Federalists came under heavy attack because of their omission of a Bill of Rights in the original Constitution.

Today it seems strange to us that the founders should not have included a basic statement about the rights that the government would be forbidden to ever infringe upon. The original Constitution protects relatively few rights. It guarantees each state a republican form of government, requires jury trials in federal cases, and prohibits ex post facto laws—laws that make criminal an act that was not criminal when it was committed. But, despite proposals during the Constitutional Convention that they add a Bill of Rights, the founders rejected the idea that they make such a list of guaranteed protections. For one thing, they argued, the federal government they had created dealt only with national questions; the rights of American citizens were better protected by the individual states. Others feared that once certain rights had been enshrined in the Constitution, it would be possible to interpret it so that only those rights were protected. (These concerns eventually led to the Ninth and Tenth Amendments being included in the Constitution.)

However, in their campaign to get the Constitution ratified, several of the Federalists eventually promised to give consideration to passing a federal Bill of Rights as soon as the Constitution had been approved. James Madison, who was elected to the first U.S. Congress to meet under the new Constitution, took it upon himself to fulfill this promise, apparently having been convinced that such a step was necessary. He drew up a list of seventeen amendments, which was eventually whittled down to twelve. Of these twelve, ten were eventually ratified by the states and became the Bill of Rights. (The second of Madison's proposed amendments, which prohibits a pay raise for congressmen from going into effect until after the next congressional election, was recently ratified as the Twenty-seventh Amendment.)

These ten amendments, of which Madison was the chief author, sum up the founders' basic beliefs about

The Bill of Rights has had more influence on the lives of ordinary American citizens than almost any other part of the Constitution.

what was necessary to ensure a healthy democratic society. The First Amendment, for example, guarantees all sorts of freedom of expression—freedom of speech, of the press, of religion, and of assembly—that were considered vital in light of the colonists' experience with the British government, which had often restricted these rights before the Revolution.

The Second and Third Amendments were another legacy of the colonists' struggle against the British; they guarantee the right to bear arms and the freedom from having to house soldiers in civilian houses during peacetime. The first right was considered vital if the citizens were to keep their ability to resist tyranny as they had when the British army had begun to attack them. The second recalled a particularly detested practice of the British government. Forcing the colonists to house and feed a soldier not only cost them money, but the soldier was expected to spy on the family that kept him and could even arrest the family if they held views against the government.

The Fifth Amendment protects the rights of citizens to refuse to incriminate themselves (that is, they cannot be forced to give evidence that might cause them to be convicted of a crime). It also states that the federal government must get an indictment from a grand jury (a special panel of citizens that decides if there is enough evidence that a person has committed a crime to charge him or her with it) before putting a person on trial, and it ensures a person the freedom from being tried more than once for the same crime (known as the double jeopardy clause) and the right to a full and fair trial, which is called due process. In addition, the Fifth Amendment also guarantees that the government will not take land or property away from people without giving them fair compensation.The Fourth Amendment, which guarantees the freedom of a citizen from illegal searches and seizures, is covered at length in the latter part of this book.

The Sixth Amendment guarantees the accused a speedy trial, an impartial jury made up of people who inhabit the region the crime was committed in, and the right of the accused to confront his or her accusers during the trial. It also guarantees the right to force witnesses who can aid in the accused's defense to testify, and the right of the accused person to have a lawyer (usually known as counsel) at trial.

The Seventh Amendment makes sure that in any civil case where the amount being sued for is greater than twenty dollars, a person is given the right to have a trial by jury. The Eighth Amendment prohibits cruel and unusual punishment.

James Madison

The great Kentucky senator Henry Clay called James Madison, "after Washington, our greatest statesman," and the career of this notable Virginian certainly supports Clay's claim.

James Madison was born in 1751 and died in 1836. During his lifetime, he held nearly every important post in the U.S. government, from member of Congress to president of the United States. Even more important, he helped to create that very government.

A member of Congress under the Articles of Confederation, Madison clearly saw the need for reform. He was one of the leaders of the Constitutional Convention and the author of many of the basic concepts of the U.S. Constitution. His efforts in Virginia helped secure its crucial ratification of the new document. During this time, he promised to write a national Bill of Rights, which he did as a member of the first Congress.

Madison was later Thomas Jefferson's secretary of state and president of the United States from 1808 to 1816. During his term as president, he led the country in its second successful struggle against Great Britain, the War of 1812. After leaving the presidency, he retired to Virginia, where he ran the University of Virginia and worked to end slavery. His notes on the Constitutional Convention, published after his death, are our best source of information on the writing of the Constitution.

The Ninth and Tenth Amendments are somewhat unusual—they do not contain any specific rights but merely remind us that the rights contained within the Bill of Rights are not the only rights of citizens of the United States. In fact, they state that those rights not specifically given to the federal government remain with the states or the people. Neither of these amendments has been the source of many court decisions. They remain important, however, as the basic principles held by the authors of the Constitution.

The intent of the Bill of Rights, it should be noted, was to protect the majority from the minority, as it had been the minority of the British rulers that had oppressed the majority of American colonists. Furthermore, the founders were far more concerned that the government might oppress the citizens of the United States than they were with protecting the rights of people who were the subjects of discrimination.

The debate over the ratification of the Constitution had shown that this was one of the primary concerns of the people of the day, and that protection from a strong central government had been the chief request of the Antifederalists. In time, however, this would change, and the Bill of Rights would come into its own as a protection for all the people of the United States. Eventually, the Bill of Rights would become a powerful instrument that would restore freedom to people who had long been denied it, as well as destroy the practices of many local governments that were in conflict with the very ideals of the American Revolution.

To understand how this happened—how the Constitution and the Bill of Rights underwent a second birth—we must turn to the events both before and after the Civil War and understand how that bloody catastrophe transformed America.

3 The Supreme Court and the Bill of Rights Before the Civil War

The judicial branch of the federal government is the Supreme Court. In all matters of federal law—whether a dispute between two states, a conflict between a state and the federal government, or simply the application of federal criminal law—the Supreme Court has the final say. It acts as the court of final appeal for lower federal courts. It decides certain cases of international law involving the United States government. But the most powerful ability the Supreme Court possesses is judicial review, the ability to decide whether or not a law complies with the Constitution. Since a law that does not do so must be stricken down, the decisions of the Supreme Court have nationwide importance.

The Constitution does not directly mention this crucial power of the Supreme Court. It owes its existence largely to one man, the nation's fourth chief justice, John Marshall.

Marshall served longer as chief justice than any other person and was one of the most influential justices in

American history. During his tenure as chief justice, he made a number of rulings in important cases that affected how courts interpreted the Constitution long after his death.

One of these was the case that established the very existence of the power of judicial review: *Marbury v. Madison* (1803). The case involved a dispute between William Marbury and the federal government. Marbury had been appointed justice of the peace for Washington, DC by President John Adams. Before he could be sworn in, however, Thomas Jefferson became president, and his new secretary of state, James Madison (the author of the Bill of Rights) refused to give Marbury the job. Marbury asked the Supreme Court to compel Madison to give him the job, under a provision of the Judiciary Act of 1789.

John Marshall, who in a strange twist of fate had been President Adams's secretary of state and thus the man who had, for unknown reasons, failed to complete Marbury's appointment in the first place, ruled that the Constitution did not allow him to compel Madison to give Marbury the job. Then he went beyond the facts of the case and ruled that the Judiciary Act of 1789 itself was unconstitutional and had to be stricken down. In another part of his decision, he claimed that only the judicial branch of the government had the power to decide on a law's constitutionality.

The basis of his decision was Article VI of the Constitution, which proclaims that the U.S. Constitution is the supreme law of the United States (this part of Article VI is known as the Supremacy Clause), and valid even when state or federal law contradicts it. Marshall's ruling in

Marbury v. Madison helped to make clear how this clause was to be enforced. Prior to this case, many people, such as Thomas Jefferson, had felt that the states were best equipped to combat unconstitutional laws by "nullifying" (refusing to obey) unconstitutional laws. Others felt that the best method was for juries to refuse to convict people accused of breaking an unconstitutional law. Marshall, however, wanted the power of enforcing the Supremacy Clause to lie within the federal government. He was a committed Federalist who believed in a strong central government. At the same time, he took pains to make sure that judicial review was and would remain a power of the judicial branch, which was impartial, unlike Congress or the president.

Marshall's strong personality left its stamp on the Supreme Court and the way the Constitution was interpreted. In a case with issues similar to *Marbury v. Madison*, Marshall again made clear that only the federal government had the authority to interpret the U.S. Constitution. The case, *Martin v. Hunter's Lessee* (1816), questioned whether or not Virginia state judges could rule on whether or not a state law violated the U.S. Constitution. Marshall decided that they could not. Only federal judges could rule on a law's constitutionality. This was a vital ruling, for without it the Constitution could have ended up being interpreted in many different ways in different states.

Another case decided by Marshall ruled on the scope of the federal government and the Constitution's—specifically, the Bill of Rights'—protections for American citizens. *Barron v. Baltimore* was about the confiscation by the city of Baltimore of a man's wharf for use in building a public-works project. John Barron, feeling that he had not

Structure of the Supreme Court

Although the number of justices who sit on the Supreme Court has been nine for more than a hundred years, neither this nor any other number of justices is mentioned in the Constitution. Congress, however, has the power to decide how many justices should be part of the Supreme Court. In 1789, this number was set at six: one chief justice and five associate justices; since then, it has been as high as ten. Once appointed, justices serve for life (or until they retire) unless impeached and removed from office. Each justice, including the chief justice, must be confirmed by the Senate before he or she can sit on the court, even if—as was the case with the current chief justice, William H. Rehnquist—the person is already an associate justice.

Congress gradually added new associate justices to the Court: six in 1807, eight in 1837, and nine (making a total of ten justices on the court) in 1864. When a vacancy opened up in 1866, no one was appointed to fill it, bringing the total of justices back down to nine, where it has remained ever since. An odd number of justices is considered superior, as it prevents a tie from occurring.

Only in the twentieth century have any justices not been both white and male. The first African American justice was Thurgood Marshall, who served from 1967 to 1991; the first woman appointed to the Court was Sandra Day O'Connor, who has served from 1981 to the present.

John Marshall, the fourth chief justice of the Supreme Court, presided over *Marbury v. Madison* (1803) and other crucial cases that set a precedent for a balance of powers in the nation's government.

received adequate compensation for losing his wharf, appealed to the Supreme Court, arguing that the "takings" clause of the Fifth Amendment protected all U.S. citizens from having the government take their property without offering proper compensation, no matter if it was a state government or the federal government.

The Supreme Court ruled against him. Marshall held that the Bill of Rights applied only to the federal government, not to the states. His ruling was correct to the letter of the law; the Bill of Rights had been created to protect the citizens from the actions of an oppressive federal government and limited only its powers, not the powers of the individual states.

This ruling, however, closed off any appeal under the Bill of Rights for unfair actions taken by the states. A state law could enable the state to take actions directly prohibited by the Bill of Rights, provided the law did not conflict with the constitution of the state it was written in. While many states had individual bills of rights that granted even more protections than the federal Bill of Rights, the potential for great injustice still existed at the state level. Racial and ethnic prejudice, supported by local laws, existed in many places, and tensions over the divisive issue of slavery were plaguing the young republic. Soon they would erupt into conflict, a conflict that would forever change the way the Constitution interacted with the lives of the citizens of the United States.

4 The Fourteenth and Fourth Amendments

For four years between 1861 and 1865, America was plunged into a vicious and bloody conflict that tore apart the fabric of the nation. The arguments over slavery and the role of the states in the federal government, which had become more and more strident over the years, finally exploded into violence. When the war finally ended, over 600,000 soldiers and many thousands of civilians were dead. In the South, millions of dollars of property damage left the region economically devastated for years to come.

The Civil War did more than cause death and destruction; it also permanently changed the way the people of the United States interacted with the federal government. Prior to the war, the national government had virtually no effect on the everyday lives of most citizens; about the only time the people dealt with the government was when they mailed a letter. But the war changed all that. The largest and most devastating conflict in United States history, the Civil War caused the federal government to take an active role in the lives of the people of the United States. Millions of men served in the military, directly employed by the government. With a desperate need for supplies of all sorts (the war cost the federal government more than a million dollars a day), companies all across the United States now found the government to be their customer. And with unrest sweeping many areas, the government proclaimed martial law in some places, bringing the people who lived there directly under federal rule.

As far back as the Constitutional Convention, the issues that would eventually provoke the bloodiest war in American history had divided the nation. The southern states, with an economy based on plantation farming and smaller populations than the northern states, wanted a weak federal government that would give the states great leeway to steer their own course. The northern states, however, were rapidly becoming industrialized, and they favored intervention by the federal government in the form of tariffs that would make their manufactured products sell better in the United States and federal money for projects such as roads, canals, and railways that would aid in the expansion of their factories. These programs were often blocked by the southern states, resulting in a series of compromises that managed to pull the country from the brink of disaster several times.

By the late 1850s, the most divisive issue of all—southern reliance on slavery to maintain its plantation economy—finally destroyed all hope of further compromise. Resolving the issue of slavery forced the federal government to make unprecedented intrusions into local government and forever changed the relationship between the federal government and ordinary Americans.

In 1863, President Abraham Lincoln issued his Emancipation Proclamation. This freed all the slaves in those regions of the Confederacy still not controlled by the Union. It did not, however, include the loyal border states, such as Maryland, where slavery was still legal. Congress decided to end all debate on the question by passing an amendment that would make slavery illegal throughout the United States. Furthermore, as it was clear that the freedmen in the South would still face prejudice from the governments of the region, it added two other amendments designed to protect the rights of these new citizens. Together, these three "Reconstruction amendments" greatly expanded the protections guaranteed by the federal government.

The Thirteenth Amendment abolished slavery, and the Fifteenth guaranteed the right to vote to all (male) persons born within the United States. But in many ways, the most important amendment was the Fourteenth Amendment—the "due process" amendment.

As we have seen, the Supreme Court in *Barron v. Baltimore* had ruled that the Bill of Rights did not apply to actions taken by state or local governments. Knowing, however, that the governments in the former Confederacy were likely to try to restore the freedmen to a condition where they had no rights at all, the authors of the Fourteenth Amendment decided to expand the protections against this kind of discrimination. To do so, however, they had to make some radical changes not only in the Constitution but also in the way it had been interpreted.

There are five sections to the Fourteenth Amendment. Sections two through four deal with the situation in the

United States at the end of the Civil War; specifically, they change the way that the population of the states had been counted for purposes of representation in Congress (slaves had counted only as three-fifths of a person); they make it illegal for former Confederate government officials or military personnel to hold a federal office; and they refuse to honor the debts run up by the Confederate government. The fifth section gives Congress the power to enforce any of the provisions of the previous four sections. But the first section is the most radical and far-reaching part of the amendment.

There are three very important changes to the Constitution contained in this section. First, it makes all persons born in the United States citizens. This is important in light of the second change: The states are forbidden to restrict the rights and privileges of U.S. citizens. Finally, each state must provide "due process" (regular procedures designed to guarantee fairness) before depriving a citizen of life, liberty, or property, and each state must provide "equal protection" under its laws for all citizens. This meant, in principle, that the same rules of due process must apply to all the citizens of a state. Furthermore, since all U.S. citizens were entitled to the protections of the Bill of Rights in federal matters, the Fourteenth Amendment should have therefore extended those protections to state and local actions, overturning the rule established by *Barron v. Baltimore*.

Unfortunately, it would take a hundred years for this principle to be upheld. Conservative Supreme Courts consistently limited the extension of the guarantees of the Bill of Rights; for most of the nineteenth century, the Fourteenth

Amendment was used by businesses to overturn legislation that they felt impeded them. However, the Civil War and the Reconstruction amendments had forever changed the nature of the United States. A massive effort by the federal government had succeeded in keeping the nation united; millions had discovered a patriotism that extended beyond their home town or state. And now the government had the power to intervene even at the local level to protect its citizens, although it would require a long and hard fight for this ultimate change to finally take place.

It was not until the twentieth century that many of the rights guaranteed in the Bill of Rights were applied to the states as well. This process, called incorporation (when a protection from the Bill of Rights is found to apply to the states as well, it is said to be incorporated against the states), was a slow one, frequently requiring the reversal of previous Supreme Court rulings. Many people were opposed to the whole process, feeling that incorporation violated the spirit of American federalism. What was the point of having separate state governments, they argued, if the federal government could step in and change such things as how local police officers interrogated suspects? Other individuals, however, argued that the Fourteenth Amendment demanded just this sort of intervention. For far too long, they said, state and local governments had been allowed to violate the rights of their citizens in ways that the national government could not. It made an even greater mockery of American federalism for states to have fewer protections than the national government extended. In the end, the latter view prevailed, and much of the Bill of Rights has been extended to protect people at the state and local level.

How to Appeal a Case to the Supreme Court

The Supreme Court decides relatively few cases directly. Most of its decisions involve appeals made by the losing side of a case decided by a lower court, but first, certain conditions must be met.

The Court can hear appeals from lower federal courts. It also can decide an appeal sent to it after the state court has ruled in a case. In both instances, however, the Court must decide if there is a federal question involved in the case, one relating to a treaty, act of Congress, or issue of constitutional law. By their very nature, appeals from federal courts involve federal questions. Another way the Court can hear an appeal has existed since 1925, when Congress authorized writs of certiorari. A writ of certiorari allows the losing side of a case to petition the Court directly to hear a case. If four justices vote to hear the case, then certiorari is granted and the Court will decide the issue.

Both sides then present written statements that set forth what they believe the case is about and cite previous rulings by the Supreme Court or other courts in similar cases. Each side also has the chance to speak to the Court directly. At the end of the process, the justices consider each argument and then take a vote. The side that the majority of justices vote for wins. The justices then prepare an opinion, a written statement of why they came to that decision. Other justices who agree with the decision, but have different reasons than the justice preparing the majority opinion, may also write their own opinions. The minority may also prepare an opinion that states why it thinks the majority ruled incorrectly.

Some rights, however, have never been incorporated against the states. The Second Amendment right to bear arms is one example; local governments have the right to regulate firearms however they choose. Another unincorporated right is the Third Amendment: freedom from the quartering of troops in the homes of civilians in peacetime, which has never been the basis of any Supreme Court decision.

As the federal government expanded its power and influence, the Supreme Court likewise expanded its interpretation of the Bill of Rights. During the intense debates over civil rights in the 1950s and 60s, the Court used the Fourteenth Amendment and the Bill of Rights to overturn state action considered prejudicial or restrictive. It was during this period that the Fourteenth Amendment finally began to fulfill its purpose, providing a shield to those who were victims of their own state governments.

Much of the Fourteenth Amendment work was done during the period of time that Earl Warren was chief justice of the Supreme Court. The "Warren Court" (1954–1969) was responsible for the incorporation of much of the Bill of Rights. Far more liberal than almost any other Court in U.S. history, the Warren Court sometimes drew severe criticism from people who felt that its rulings—especially those dealing with searches and seizures and other rights of the accused—had placed too many restrictions on the police. During his successful campaign for president in 1968, Richard Nixon accused the Court of having been "soft on crime" and promised to appoint new justices who would issue rulings in favor of the police.

Nixon's appointment to replace Earl Warren in 1969 was Warren Burger. More conservative than his predecessor, Burger

State of New Jersey,
County of HUNTERDON } ss.

Anna Hauptmann of the City of Trenton in the County of Mercer and State of New Jersey, upon ~~xxxxoath~~ information and belief complains and says that on the or about first day of March A. D., 1932, at the township of East Amwell in the County ~~aforesaid~~ of Hunterdon one Paul Wendel did feloniously break and enter the premises of one Charles A. Lindbergh, and did steal, take, carry away and kidnap the male infant, Charles A. Lindbergh, Jr., a child of the then-age of twenty months, all of which conduct is contrary to the statute in such case made and provided,

Wherefore, She prays that the said Paul Wendel may be apprehended and held to answer to said Complaint, and dealt with as law and justice may require.

Subscribed and sworn to at Flemington the third day of April A. D., 1936, before me,

Geo. Webster
Justice of the Peace.

Anna Hauptmann

The Fourth Amendment of the Constitution restricted the power of the government to make "unreasonable" searches and seizures.

did indeed moderate several of the rulings of the Warren Court, although there were enough liberal justices remaining that few of the Warren Court decisions could be overturned. Burger's replacement, appointed by President Ronald Reagan in 1986, was the even more conservative William Rehnquist, the current chief justice. Although the Rehnquist Court has reversed several parts of the "Warren Revolution," it has not overturned its most controversial decisions.

Why a Fourth Amendment?

The American legal system owes much to the British. Over the 150 years of the American colonial experience, the laws, customs, and institutions of government were either British or based on British models. It was, in fact, a source of pride for the colonists, for they held that the British system was the finest in the world and guaranteed its citizens more freedom than any other nation in Europe. Before the Revolutionary War, many of the future founders simply wanted their rights as Englishmen to be acknowledged. Yet curiously enough, the Fourth Amendment was specifically drafted in response to a British custom of long standing: the general warrant.

A general warrant was a document that allowed government officials to arrest and search any person, or search any place and seize anything they found. While there were some restrictions on the practice in English common law, its power could be truly terrifying. A general warrant gave the government the unlimited right to break into a person's home or place of business and take his or her private papers and other intimate possessions, regardless of whether or not they had any bearing on the crime of which the person had been accused. Another kind of warrant, called a writ of assistance, made it possible for government officials to demand the assistance of bystanders or other government officials.

The English prided themselves on their parliamentary institutions and the concept of limited government they had enshrined in the Magna Carta. But the general warrants were frequently used as a tool of the government against those who disagreed with it. During the upheavals in English society between 1500 and 1700, the warrants were used against Catholic dissenters and opponents of the government. People who were charged with executing the warrants were frequently accused of corruption, as it was believed that they kept items they had seized for themselves.

By the 1690s, however, political changes in England had resulted in Parliament having much greater power than

Precedent: *Stare Decisis*

The Latin phrase *stare decisis* means "stand by what is decided." It is one of the most important principles in American law. Basically, it means that when deciding a case, a judge must consider decisions in similar cases that have been tried before and consider himself or herself bound by their precedent.

Without precedent, different judges could rule differently even in cases that are nearly identical. Precedent also gives a judge guidelines as to what is fair in cases without prior precedent; by comparing the penalties or rules of cases of similar severity, he or she can come to a ruling that is both fair and appropriate within current law.

Although the Supreme Court weighs precedent very heavily, it is not bound by any precedent, even its own. In fact, the Court may decide that earlier rulings in a given matter were incorrect and reverse itself, handing down a new decision that then becomes precedent for all lower courts. The reversal of a previous ruling is frequently a momentous occasion. The Court may also decide to break with precedent but note that the case it is deciding is different enough from the original decision that precedent is not affected. More common than complete reversal is a decision by the Court that merely clarifies previous decisions.

had previously been the case, and the use of general warrants began to decline. Also, British legal theorists such as the famous Sir Edward Coke—who was known for being liberal-minded—began to urge that the general warrant violated the Magna Carta and British common law. In fact, the Magna Carta has nothing to say about general warrants, but in time the argument came to be accepted by many.

Despite these changes, and Parliament's growing authority, general warrants continued to be used both in England and the American colonies. However, in America, where many of the colonies had been founded with the goal of greater religious freedom, the general warrants were almost never used to persecute religious minorities, as had been the case in England. Furthermore, in some of the northern colonies, experiments with a different kind of warrant, the specific warrant, had begun. Unlike a general warrant, a specific warrant names a particular place to be searched and the charges that the person is being accused of; more important, it limits what may be seized to only those items that are evidence of the crime the person is accused of committing.

Massachusetts was the first colony to use specific warrants, and although it later reverted to using general warrants, the principles behind the specific warrant remained part of public consciousness. In 1760, when the death of King George II meant that the warrants he had issued would expire in six months, the high court of Massachusetts heard the Paxton case, where a customs official petitioned for a new general warrant. He was opposed by James Otis Jr., a Boston lawyer who argued that general warrants were illegal under the Magna Carta and common law, as well as the "higher law" of freedom and liberty. Otis eventually lost his case because his defense, while impassioned, did in fact contain many mistakes and misconceptions; but his fiery arguments did much to increase the colonists' growing sense of separation from the British. John Adams, one of the principal signers of the Declaration of Independence and later the second president of the United States, watched the trials as a young man and later claimed that the American independence movement was born then and there.

However, shortly after the Paxton trial, a series of cases known as the Wilkes cases took place in England. John Wilkes had published a paper that was critical of the government, and general warrants had been used to arrest him and almost fifty other people. The government searched houses, seizing thousands of books and personal papers. Wilkes then proceeded to sue any and all of the officials connected to the case. At issue was whether the government could use a general warrant in an area where there was no law allowing them to (known as a warrant based on statute) but merely the custom of issuing warrants in similar cases. The judge in the case, Charles Pratt, found that such warrants were illegal under the Magna Carta. In a later case, he found that personal papers could not be seized and used against a person, as that would force the person to incriminate himself.

The Wilkes cases came during the time that the British government was beginning to try to take more direct control not only of the colonies' governments but of their economies, too. General warrants had long been used to enforce taxes on manufactured or imported goods; now that the British government was increasing these taxes, it began to issue more general warrants to enforce them.

The colonists objected strenuously. Although the Wilkes cases had been found to apply only to warrants based on custom—which the warrants issued to enforce the tax laws were not—the principle of restricting searches and seizures seemed to have been upheld by the decisions in the trial. Pamphlets and newspaper accounts of the cases were printed throughout the colonies. Resistance to the principle of the general warrant became almost the same thing as resistance to the British. During the Revolutionary War, when each state drafted its own constitution, eight of them rejected the entire concept.

Even with independence won, however, some forms of general warrants continued to survive in America. Because of this, and because of fears of the new, stronger federal government—created by the Constitution—there was a call for a protection against this powerful tool of government in the Bill of Rights. James Madison's response was to draft an amendment that allowed only specific warrants. In time, this brief addition to the Constitution would give Americans a greater freedom from searches and seizures than the citizens of any other country in the world.

5 An Overview of Fourth Amendment Protections

The Fourth Amendment protects people from "unreasonable" searches of their persons, houses, papers, and effects. But what constitutes an unreasonable search? What guidelines exist constitutionally to help determine whether or not a search is prohibited by the Fourth Amendment?

The text of the amendment itself offers no definition of either a "reasonable" or "unreasonable" search. Some have argued that this means that the interpretation of the amendment has to be guided by common law, and that the opinion of a judge decides whether or not a search is unreasonable. Others have argued that the amendment merely provides a person who has been the victim of an unreasonable search the ability to sue the officials who searched him or her.

However, for the most part, judges and the Supreme Court have relied on the next part of the amendment, which requires that warrants only be issued with "probable cause," and that they be specific, limited warrants that name the person or place to be searched. According to this understanding, a search can only be considered reasonable if a warrant has been issued. However, the Court has recognized that there are circumstances when the public good requires that a search be performed without a warrant. Determining the precise circumstances in which a warrantless search can be "reasonable" has always spurred great controversy.

One important factor to note is that searches conducted by a private citizen are not covered by the Fourth Amendment. It is only when the government steps in to search a person that his or her constitutional protections are triggered. In the 1921 case of *Burdeau v. McDowell*, the Court ruled that the Fourth Amendment did not protect J.C. McDowell, who, after being fired by his employers, had had his office safe opened up and the contents of it and his desk given to the federal Justice Department. This evidence was used to convict McDowell of mail fraud, and he appealed to the Supreme Court to overturn the conviction based on his Fourth Amendment rights. The Court refused to do so, noting that he could still sue his former employers for damages.

One exception to the warrant requirement is the "plain view" exception. Basically, this allows police who are lawfully in an area to seize evidence not specifically covered by a warrant. For example, if a policeman were to witness two people taking illegal drugs in public, he would not need a warrant to arrest them and seize the drugs. Likewise, if in searching a house under a warrant to find the weapon used to kill someone in a robbery a policewoman saw the stolen goods lying around, she could seize them, even though they were not specifically included in the warrant. However, the items must be in plain view, not hidden inside a drawer or locked in a closet.

There are two basic steps necessary to obtain a warrant to search or arrest someone: probable cause and a neutral magistrate. Both are required in order to get a warrant that does not violate the Fourth Amendment.

Probable cause means that there is enough evidence to convince a magistrate—an official such as a judge charged with administering the laws—that a crime has been committed by the person for whom the warrant is to be issued. In cases of search warrants, both the place to be searched and the crime that has been committed must be specifically stated. It is possible that evidence of the crime not included in the warrant, or found outside the area that the warrant was issued for, may later prove to be inadmissible as evidence at trial (See chapter 7).

Evidence used for probable cause does not have to meet the tougher standards of evidence used at trial. However, it must be made under "oath or affirmation" according to the Fourth Amendment, and it must be supported by facts. In other words, the government cannot get a warrant just because they suspect a person has committed a crime; they must have other evidence that supports the idea that not only was a crime committed, but the person they are investigating could have committed it. On the other hand, hearsay evidence—testimony by people who did not actually observe the event they are describing, but merely heard about it from a third person—can be used to get a search warrant, even though such evidence cannot be used at trial. However, in the 1978 case of *Franks v. Delaware*, a warrant obtained by lying to the judge or magistrate was ruled to be unconstitutional.

Warrants are only necessary if a person does not consent to a search. That is, the police may always ask a person if they can search him or her or his or her area. It is only when that person refuses to allow them to do so that the police must get a warrant. However, in the 1973 case of *Schneckloth v. Bustamonte*, the Court ruled that the police, although they must ask, do not have to inform the person that he or she has the right to refuse to allow them to search. This decision, reached during the Burger Court, seemed to fly in the face of Warren Court decisions such as *Miranda v. Arizona*, which required that a person be informed of all their constitutional rights when being questioned by police. In 1974, the Court further found that one occupant of a house may consent to a search of the building, even if the other occupant is not there to give his or her consent—and any evidence found against the suspected person is admissible in court.

Crucial to the warrant process is the concept of the neutral magistrate. In other words, the party that grants the warrant must not have an interest in the case. In general, this means that a judge must be used to get a warrant, as they are charged with being impartial, and are not part of the police or prosecutor's department. This was emphasized by the Court's decision in the 1971 case of *Coolidge v. New Hampshire*, where a warrant had been issued by a state official who was also the chief prosecutor of the case. The Court threw out all the evidence gathered under this warrant.

On the other hand, there is no constitutional requirement that the magistrate be a judge or even a lawyer. The 1972 case of *Shadwick v. City of Tampa, Fla.* found that a municipal court clerk could issue a warrant for municipal

Earl Warren

Earl Warren (1891–1974) was one of the most active and influential chief justices in Supreme Court history.

Before becoming the chief justice of the Supreme Court, Warren had spent more than thirty years in public office, most famously as governor of California (1943–53). In 1953, he was appointed chief justice of the Supreme Court by President Dwight D. Eisenhower. When Warren's rulings as chief justice turned out to be much more liberal than the conservative Eisenhower had wanted, he called the appointment "the worst mistake of my life." Others would dispute that, however.

Warren made many rulings that affected race relations in the United States. One of the most famous of these was the decision in *Brown v. Board of Education* (1954), which overturned the "separate but equal" doctrine that had prevailed for over sixty years, and ordered the desegregation of public schools.

Warren's Court also made many rulings that profoundly changed the rights of the accused in the United States. In *Miranda v. Arizona* (1966), the Court found that police could not question a person unless he or she was made to understand all of his or her constitutionally protected rights. This is the source of the famous Miranda Rights that the police must read to any person they arrest ("You have the right to remain silent," etc.). In 1961, the decision in *Mapp v. Ohio* expanded Fourth Amendment protections to everyone in the United States.

Earl Warren died in 1974. His legacy of expanding the protections of the Bill of Rights, however, remains substantially unchanged.

offenses. However, the magistrate in question must normally be involved in deciding cases involving crimes described in the warrant; therefore, for serious criminal offenses, judges usually are required to issue a search warrant.

The Fourth Amendment protects people from unreasonable searches and seizures. It does this primarily by requiring the government to get a warrant before they can even begin to make a search. However, how can the Fourth Amendment protect a person if a warrant is wrongly issued, or if the police overstep the restrictions of the warrant? What recourse does a person who is being tried under those conditions have under the Fourth Amendment? The answer to these questions involves some of the most controversial decisions made by the Supreme Court, which are the subject of the next chapter.

6 The Fourth Amendment at Trial

In the previous chapter, we explored the fundamental requirements that have to be met for a search to be legal under the Fourth Amendment. The evolution of these protections, however, took many years and involved several complex Supreme Court decisions.

The questions that the Court was forced to address were these: How can the rules of evidence, the guidelines for whether or not a piece of evidence can be used in a trial, be constructed in order to conform to the Fourth Amendment? And what can be done to guarantee fairness when the government has violated the Fourth Amendment, even without meaning to?

Prior to 1961, the cases that had to conform to the Fourth Amendment were all federal cases. It was not until the landmark decision in *Mapp v. Ohio* that the Fourth Amendment was found to apply to the states as well as the federal government.

The first major Fourth Amendment decision was the 1886 case of *Boyd v. United States*. This case involved a supplier of plate glass, E.A. Boyd, who had been contracted to make glass for several federal buildings in Philadelphia. In return for discounting their price to the government, the Boyds had asked to be allowed to import the glass without paying the special tax, called a duty, which was normally required.

However, the government soon had cause to suspect that the Boyds were actually cheating by importing more glass than they needed for the government contract, as a way of getting around the duty on the glass they used on other jobs. The government went to court, demanding that the Boyds forfeit the contract. During the trial, the judge ordered the Boyds to show all their invoices for the glass they had imported; the Boyds protested, but eventually gave in, and were convicted. They then appealed the decision on the basis of their Fourth Amendment right of freedom from unreasonable seizures and their Fifth Amendment right against self-incrimination.

In considering the case, the Supreme Court had to carefully examine both amendments and decide what should be done if they had been violated. In this case, the Court sided with the Boyds. By ordering them to produce the papers, the judge had indeed violated both their Fourth and Fifth Amendment rights. In fact, the Court said that the two amendments had much in common with each other, for clearly the right to be "secure" in one's person or dwelling means that a person should not be forced to give up evidence that might be incriminating. The Court ordered not only that the conviction be reversed, but also that a new trial take place, one in which the incriminating evidence could not be used.

Another major precedent came out of the 1914 case of *Weeks v. United States,* when for the first time the Court laid down guidelines for the kinds of searches that could be permitted under the Fourth Amendment. A series of further decisions soon established two rules of evidence, one of which is still used today (and in many ways is the most restrictive such rule in the world), the other of which was abandoned in the 1970s: the exclusionary rule and the "mere evidence" rule.

The Exclusionary Rule

In the *Boyd* case, the Court had ordered a new trial to remedy the use of improperly acquired evidence. However, this solution was impractical on a large scale; the involved expenses alone would be too great, not to mention the way it would clog the nation's court systems. To remedy this problem, the Court created the exclusionary rule in *Weeks v. United States*.

The case involved the arrest of Fremont Weeks and the search of his home, all without a warrant. On the basis of evidence resulting from these searches, he was convicted at trial and appealed his case to the Supreme Court, under his Fourth Amendment rights.

The Court not only overturned his conviction, but adopted a controversial new policy: evidence that had been seized in violation of the Fourth Amendment could not be used at trial. This meant that during a trial, a defendant could move that evidence being used by the government be excluded, if the defense felt that it had been acquired illegally. This had profound effects on the American justice system.

Just as *Boyd* had noted the close relationship between the Fourth and Fifth Amendments, the Court would soon find that evidence that would violate the Fifth Amendment protection from self-incrimination (and, eventually, even the Sixth Amendment right to counsel) had to be excluded as well. In 1920, the Court ruled that all evidence illegally seized was inadmissible, even photocopies. However, some evidence that cannot be used to establish that a person has committed a crime can still be used to "impeach" his or her credibility, meaning to show that the person has lied on the stand. And only the person whose rights were violated can move to exclude the results of a search or seizure.

At this point, the rules of evidence the Court had created, including the exclusionary rule, still only applied to the federal government. This was affirmed again in the 1949 case of *Wolf v. Colorado*. This case involved only actions taken on a state level; evidence used in the case, however, would have been excluded in a federal court. However, the Supreme Court did not overturn the conviction. Their decision did find, however, that the Fourteenth Amendment extended the Fourth Amendment protections to the states. However, the Court ruled that the states were not required to obey the exclusionary rule, provided that they had other means of preventing illegal searches. In fact, at the time, only seventeen states had exclusionary rules similar to those the Court created in the *Weeks* decision. Indeed, only if a state had enacted laws allowing for searches and seizures in violation of these guidelines would the Fourteenth Amendment allow the case to be overturned. This apparent contradiction was not firmly resolved until the *Mapp v. Ohio* decision. However, cases where the police clearly overstepped the bounds of decency could still be overturned under the Fourth Amendment. For example, in *Rochin v. California*, decided in 1952, the Court overturned the conviction of a man who had swallowed two capsules of illegal drugs rather than let the police find them on him when they came to arrest him. The police had then had his stomach pumped to recover the capsules, which were used as evidence against him. The Court found that this shocking conduct could in no way be considered "reasonable."

Another problem that *Weeks* created was the so-called "silver platter" doctrine. Basically, this allowed federal prosecutors to use evidence that would normally be inadmissible (because the searches or seizures were in violation of the federal rules of evidence) provided that it had been uncovered by state agents, acting without federal help. This is because the states were not bound by the Fourth Amendment; they could conduct illegal searches and then hand the evidence to the federal prosecutors on a "silver platter." This situation managed to exist even after the *Wolf* case found that the Fourth Amendment did indeed apply, in principle, to the states; the silver platter doctrine was not overturned until 1960.

Mapp v. Ohio

The decision in *Mapp v. Ohio* finally ended this confusion, but in doing so it created even more controversy.

In 1957, the police came to Dollree Mapp's house in Cleveland, demanding to search it for a person who was wanted for questioning in connection with a recent bombing. Rather than let them in right away, she called an attorney and then refused to let the police come in until they had a warrant. The police then left.

When they came back, they forced their way inside, waving a piece of paper they claimed was a warrant in her face. She snatched it away and stuffed it in her bosom, but the police forcibly recovered it. They then searched the house and found books, pictures, and photographs that were considered obscene under Ohio law. Dollree Mapp was arrested, tried, and convicted for possession of such materials.

Her appeal eventually reached the Supreme Court, which ruled to overturn her conviction—and also to apply the exclusionary rule to the states. Justice Tom Clark noted, in the majority opinion, that "nothing can destroy a government more quickly than its failure to observe its own laws, or worse, its disregard of the charter of its own existence...."

Since its inception, the exclusionary rule had been controversial. Often, removing one piece of evidence from the prosecution's case can completely wreck any chance of convicting a person of a crime, even if he or she is guilty. The chance that a criminal can go free because of a technicality is increased by the exclusionary rule. As Benjamin Cardozo, the famous New York judge, put it before he served as a Supreme Court justice, "the criminal is to go free because the constable has blundered."

Others, however, have said that not only does the exclusionary rule protect the highest principles of American liberty but that sometimes the guilty must be allowed to go free in order for the innocent not to be convicted. Some studies have found that the majority of cases where the exclusionary rule has been used would only have resulted in small fines.

Still, the decision in *Mapp* was highly controversial, because it forced all of the states to follow the exclusionary rule. This, along with several other Warren Court decisions of the early 60s such as *Miranda*, *Gideon*, and *Escobedo*, expanded the rights of the accused found in the Bill of Rights to the states. This led many to feel that the Court was protecting criminals at the expense of law-abiding citizens. Thus, the more conservative courts of the 1970s and 1980s refused to continue to expand the exclusionary rule, and in many places found exceptions to it. For example, the Court did not expand the exclusionary rule to include grand juries, special juries that decide whether or not to issue an indictment. An indictment is a formal statement accusing a person of committing a crime.

In 1984, two important exceptions to the exclusionary rule were permitted by the Court. The case of *United States v. Leon* addressed a curious paperwork error in California. The police had requested a warrant to search the houses and cars of several people accused of various drug crimes. On the basis of evidence seized under this warrant, the people were convicted. However, the evidence used to obtain the warrant was not technically admissible under California procedures. The question for the Court was whether or not such a technical mistake should invalidate the search.

The Court ruled that it did not. The police were acting in "good faith." They had taken the time to secure a warrant, and had no reason to suppose that the warrant was improper. Under these circumstances, the search could be considered legal.

The other important exception granted that year was "inevitable discovery." This means that if the prosecution can demonstrate that other evidence ultimately would have led the police to evidence that had been illegally seized, it would be admissible at trial.

The good faith exception of *Leon* continued to be expanded during the 1980s and 1990s. In 1987, the Court ruled that a search and seizure conducted under a law that was later declared unconstitutional was another example of the good faith provision. A similar case decided that even if the police went to the wrong apartment, a search or seizure might be considered legal if they were acting in good faith.

And in 1995, the case of *Arizona v. Evans* extended the provision to include errors by the magistrate, not the police. A search was conducted by the police under a warrant, which, although it appeared to be valid, had actually been "quashed," or suppressed. However, a computer error meant that the police were not notified in time. The Court ruled that the search was legal. Clerical errors made by the court's employees did not provide grounds for the exclusionary rule.

The "Mere Evidence" Rule

In the 1921 case of *Gouled v. United States*, the Court was asked to decide exactly what kind of evidence could be searched for under the Fourth Amendment. A friend of Felix Gouled had come to his place of business at the request of federal agents and removed several papers. These papers were later used to convict Gouled of defrauding the government with certain defense contracts.

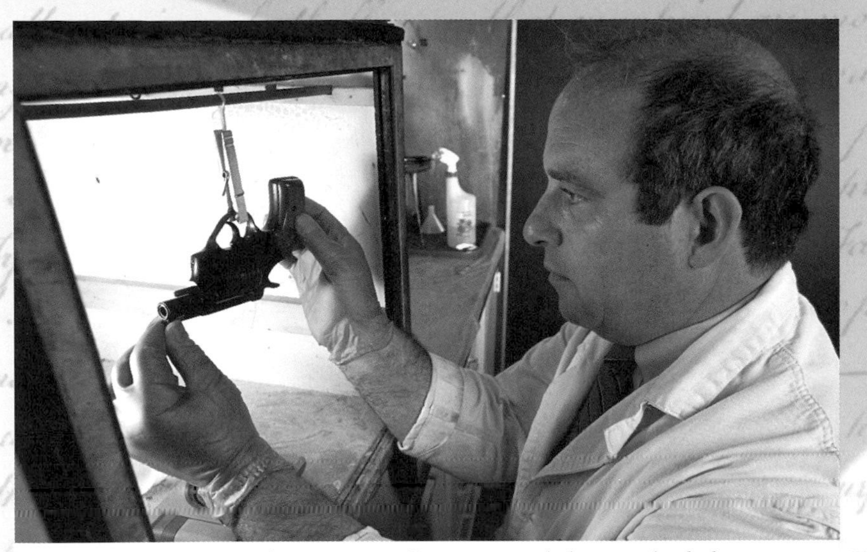

The Supreme Court has continually reassessed the standards by which evidence is judged admissible in legal proceedings.

Gouled appealed to the Supreme Court, claiming his Fourth and Fifth Amendment rights had been violated. The Court upheld this part of his defense, as the *Weeks* decision clearly seemed to apply here, since the search had been warrantless and done under false pretenses. However, it further ruled that the type of evidence used against Gouled was inadmissible as well. The documents did not relate to the crime, but merely provided evidence that it had been committed. The Court ruled that only those items that were either the "fruits or instrumentalities" of a crime could be admitted as evidence. For example, a painting stolen in a robbery could be used as evidence because it was the "fruit" of a crime; a gun used to commit murder could be evidence, since it was an "instrumentality" of the crime. But, as the Gouled decision showed, letters that merely indicated a person had committed a crime could not be used as evidence against a person.

The Court's decision was based on the theory that the Fourth Amendment also protected the property of a person. Property interests were an important subject for the Court in the nineteenth and early twentieth centuries, and the Court tended to be very conservative on this issue. In this case, they decided that the property interests of an individual were greater than the public interest of the government.

While the decision would seem to severely restrict warrants, in actual practice it did not have a great effect. Federal law never allowed warrants for "mere evidence." However, the states could still issue warrants for a broad variety of things, many only loosely connected to a crime.

The mere evidence rule also suffered from difficulties of interpretation. What might be mere evidence in one case could be an instrument in another. Because of this, in the 1967 case of *Warden v. Hayden*, the Court overturned the mere evidence rule. Police had entered Hayden's house, without a warrant, because a person who had robbed a taxi cab had been observed running into the house. When the police determined that Hayden was the only man in the house, and that eyewitness descriptions matched the clothes the robber had been wearing to those found in a washing machine in his basement, Hayden was arrested. Based on this evidence, he was convicted; but Hayden appealed to the Supreme Court, claiming that the mere evidence rule had been violated.

The Court, in an 8-1 decision, not only refused to overturn his conviction, but overturned the mere evidence rule as well. Property wasn't the main concern of the Fourth

Amendment, the Court said, but privacy. Further, the tests for determining what constituted mere evidence were impossible to keep consistent.

One effect of the reversal of the mere evidence rule was an erosion of the Fourth Amendment's protection of personal papers. Several decisions in the 1970s upheld the principle that a valid search warrant can be used to collect anything that might be considered evidence of a crime, even the business records of an attorney accused of a crime.

The Fourth Amendment has been interpreted to provide many protections to the accused, both before and during a trial. However, what protections does it provide to people who are arrested for committing a crime? When does an arrest require a warrant, and when can it be made without a warrant? And what searches are legal at the time of arrest? These questions are explored in the next chapter.

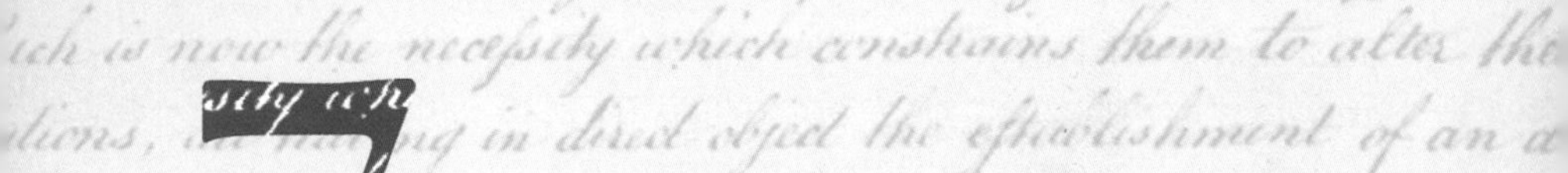

7 Arrests and Searches

The Fourth Amendment does not specifically state anything about arrests. It merely protects people from unreasonable searches and seizures. However, an arrest is, after all, a seizure: the seizure of a person. As such, Supreme Court decisions about the legality of arrests have been based on the Fourth Amendment.

That being said, the Supreme Court has not held arrests to the same standard it has held other searches and seizures. A warrantless arrest is legal under far many more circumstances than a search or seizure of evidence. However, certain basic standards still apply.

Just as probable cause is required before a judge will grant a warrant, an officer who arrests somebody without a warrant must have probable cause to believe that he or she has committed a crime. As long as probable cause exists, an arrest without a warrant will generally be upheld.

Three separate important cases illustrate various aspects of the ability of government agents to make warrantless arrests: *United States v. Watson* (1976), *United States v. Santana* (1976), and *Payton v. New York* (1980).

The first of these cases involved the warrantless arrest of a suspect in a public place. A postal inspector saw a man believed to have stolen credit cards in a restaurant, and arrested him. A search of the suspect's car found two stolen credit cards, which were used to convict him. The Supreme Court heard the case after a lower court had overturned the conviction on the basis of Watson's Fourth Amendment rights, and reinstated the conviction. The Court noted that laws specifically gave postal inspectors the right to perform warrantless arrests based on probable cause, and that doing so in this case did not mean that government agents should not generally get a warrant when arresting someone in public.

Also in 1976, the Court made a ruling about whether or not a warrantless arrest made inside a house was constitutional. In *United States v. Santana*, the police had received information that a person known as "Mom" Santana was in possession of marked money that had been used to buy drugs. When they approached her house, they saw her standing on the porch with a paper bag in her hands, at which point they rushed up, shouting "Police!" She ran inside her house, and the police followed her and arrested her. Heroin was found in the bag she was carrying, and she had some of the marked money. During the trial process, however, she moved to have the heroin and money excluded on the grounds that her arrest was illegal, since her home had been entered without a warrant.

The Court disagreed. Santana had been outside the home, exposed to public view and scrutiny. Moreover, once she was outside and observed by the police, she could not then stop them from arresting her merely by going inside. The facts of the case gave the police enough probable cause to believe a crime had been committed.

However, in 1980 the Court ruled in *Payton v. New York* that the police or government agents cannot enter a home to arrest its occupant without a warrant or the consent of the occupant. The difference in this case seems to be that in *Payton*, the action did not begin outside the house. Rather, the police, believing Payton had murdered someone, went to his apartment to arrest him. When no one answered the door, they broke it down, and used evidence found inside to convict him. In a narrow 5–4 decision, the Court found this kind of entry to be unconstitutional and beyond the scope of the police's right to make warrantless arrests.

Frisking

Frisking refers to the practice of a police officer stopping a suspicious person and searching him or her for concealed weapons. The Supreme Court has upheld this as a reasonable search under the Fourth Amendment.

One of the most important decisions in this area was the 1968 case of *Terry v. Ohio*. In this case, the Court found that the police must have some ability to search suspects for weapons, if only for their own protection. The police need not have enough probable cause to arrest the person, just enough to believe that he or she might be armed. A case decided at the same time, *Sibron v. New York*, however, demonstrated the limits of this frisking. In the *Terry* case, the officer had only patted down the suspect, and only

The courts have set guidelines on how police can search, or frisk, suspects for weapons or contraband.

reached inside the suspect's pockets when he felt a weapon. In *Sibron*, however, the officer had immediately searched the suspect's pockets, without patting him down first.

In 1993, this ruling was expanded to include any "contraband" (things, such as illegal drugs, that people are prohibited by law from possessing), provided that the officer can clearly feel the material during the frisking. This is a sort of "plain feel" exemption that complements the more basic "plain view" exemption.

Searches and Arrests

At the time of a person's arrest, the police have the ability to search the person and the area around him or her without a warrant. There are three basic reasons for this, all of which, in the eyes of the Supreme Court, have elevated the public good over the rights of the person being arrested: the chance that the person might be concealing weapons which could endanger the officers arresting him or her (see frisking); the need to prevent the escape of the person, and the need to avoid the destruction of evidence.

This custom has a long history, and the Court has not changed it, for the reasons listed above. However, for the search to be considered valid, the arrest itself must have been valid independent of any items discovered during the search.

Even so, this ability of the police is quite broad and rather undefined. What exactly are the limits to the police's power to search a person, and more importantly, the area he or she is in—especially if it is his or her home or office? At what point does such a search become unreasonable?

One of the first major cases to try and fix these limits was *Harris v. United States* (1947). In this case, the FBI had arrested a man for mail fraud in his home and then searched his entire apartment without a warrant. The search took five hours to complete, and did not uncover any evidence of mail fraud. Several draft cards that had been stolen were found, however, and Harris was convicted for their possession.

His appeal to the Supreme Court on the grounds that his Fourth Amendment rights had been infringed was rejected. Since Harris had been in control of his apartment, the Court concluded that the agents were justified in searching it. The decision was only 5–4, and Justice Frank Murphy bitterly noted in his dissenting opinion that the Court had in effect revived the hated general warrant of colonial days.

The next year, however, the case of *Trupiano v. United States* resulted in some limitations of the ability of government agents to perform searches and seizures without warrants. In

Warren Burger

Curiously, the man who was hand-picked to limit the liberal reforms of Earl Warren was named Warren Earl Burger. He was chosen by President Nixon to be the replacement for the retiring Earl Warren as chief justice of the United States Supreme Court.

Burger helped to reaffirm the famous *Miranda* decision, despite the harsh criticism of that ruling by both the president and many law-enforcement personnel throughout the country. Although his Court did indeed limit some of the decisions of the Warren Court, Burger's term was not marked by a firm stand on any particular ideology, but rather by pragmatic concerns of justice and applicability.

In 1973, the Burger Court issued a controversial decision of their own: *Roe v. Wade*, which made abortion legal throughout America. Perhaps just as controversial as the abortion aspects of the case was the assertion that there existed a right to privacy that was implied by the rights protected by the Bill of Rights, even though no such right was spelled out. This example of "loose constructionalism," or interpreting the Constitution beyond what the founders clearly laid out, was criticized by many who felt that the Constitution should be interpreted more conservatively.

Burger's term was also noted for his attention to administrative details. He helped to improve the efficiency not only of the Supreme Court, but the entire federal judiciary. After his retirement in 1986, he was chairman of the committee that planned the celebration of the Constitution's 200th anniversary in 1988. He died in 1995.

this case, federal agents had, without a warrant, arrested several men they had seen operating an illegal alcohol still. They had also then seized the still. The Court found that while the agents had probable cause to make the arrest, they did not have the right to seize the still without a warrant. The still was not a danger to their safety, nor was it apparently in danger of being destroyed. There was nothing to prevent them from getting a warrant, Justice Murphy (writing for the majority this time) noted, except their "indifference to the legal process...which the Constitution contemplated." There had to be some dividing line between the circumstances that allowed the government to seize items without a warrant at the time of arrest and circumstances under which they were required to first obtain a warrant, or else the Fourth Amendment would have no meaning. Another decision made that year made it clear that unless the officers were responding to an emergency, there had to be exceptional, exigent—requiring immediate action—circumstances for a warrantless search to be valid.

Shortly thereafter, though, the Court made yet another ruling that changed the *Trupiano* ruling that a warrant be obtained whenever doing so was practical. In *United States v. Rabinowitz*, the Court ruled that the search of the desk, file cabinets, and safe of a person who had been arrested on a valid arrest warrant in his one-room office was not unreasonable. Furthermore, it held that the failure of the government to obtain a search warrant even though they had time to do so did not make the search invalid. Thus, in overturning the "practicability" restriction on warrantless searches in the *Trupiano* ruling, the Court found that deciding whether or not a search was unreasonable when conducted without a warrant did not depend on whether or not getting a search warrant was reasonable, but whether the search itself was reasonable. This could only be determined by considering the "total atmosphere" of the case. Determining exactly what the total atmosphere of a case meant, and which circumstances would permit a warrantless search proved to be extremely difficult, and in 1969 the Court changed its position again in the case of *Chimel v. California*.

In this case, police officers had come to the house of a man with a warrant for his arrest on burglary charges. He was not home, but his wife let them in and they waited for him to return. When he did, they arrested him and then asked if they could search his house. Although he refused to give his permission, the officers searched the entire building for nearly an hour and seized many items that were used to convict him at trial.

In reversing his conviction, the Court found that while the police certainly had a right to search both the person they had arrested and the area around him or her, the search of an entire house without a search warrant was unreasonable. Only the area under the immediate control of the person they were arresting could be considered reasonable, as this was the zone where he or she might grab a weapon or try to destroy evidence. In other cases, a search warrant would have to be obtained. In doing so, they overturned not only *Rabinowitz*, but *Harris* as well, establishing a new standard of reasonableness that still stands today.

Subsequent decisions have reinforced this standard. In 1970, the Court decided that arresting a person on the street for a drug offense did not justify a search of his house without a warrant. And in 1971, in the case of *Coolidge v. New Hampshire*, the Court found that although the police had arrested a suspect inside his house, it was not reasonable for them to search a car that was in his driveway. (See chapter 8 for another aspect of the *Coolidge* case.)

One other case worth noting considered both the rights of officers to search a car without a warrant and the search of an individual without a warrant. In *United States v. Robinson*, the Court had to decide on the admissibility of drug evidence that had been discovered when an officer frisked a suspect after stopping his car. However, the police had not stopped the car because they suspected the driver of having committed a drug offense, but because he was suspected of driving with a revoked license. The Court ruled, however, that since searching the suspect, even for a traffic violation, was reasonable, the drug evidence discovered by this search was reasonable as well.

In these last two chapters, we have investigated the basic factors that determine whether or not a search can be considered reasonable under the Fourth Amendment, from the basic requirement of obtaining a warrant to the exceptions granted to the police in arresting a person. In the next few chapters, we will examine some of the specific areas that have been explored by the Court, from the rights of high school students to the shifting world of electronic surveillance.

8 Schools and the Fourth Amendment

The question of whether or not the Fourth Amendment is involved in searches of students by school officials has only been tested in the last few years. However, it touches upon some interesting questions about the nature of the Constitution and American government.

In order to maintain a safe environment and to enforce a school's disciplinary rules, school officials must occasionally search a student's locker or even their clothing. However, constitutionally this presents some problems: Is such a search a "search" the way the Fourth Amendment means it? If it is, do Fourth Amendment restrictions apply to it, or do school officials enjoy an exemption similar to that enjoyed by the police, who are allowed to perform warrantless searches under some circumstances?

And finally, what are the rights of Americans who are not yet legally "of age"? Are they citizens in the same way an adult is? Do they enjoy the same rights as an adult, or does the government enjoy more power over them, and more responsibility for their welfare as well?

The first part of these questions, whether or not the Fourth Amendment applies to students, was not addressed by the Supreme Court until 1985, with their decision in *New Jersey v. T.L.O*. A later decision, *Vernonia School District v. Acton* addressed some of the remaining concerns, but certain areas of this thorny issue still have not been addressed by the Court.

New Jersey v. T.L.O

In a New Jersey high school, a teacher found two freshmen girls smoking in the bathroom. At this school, smoking was not against the rules, but students who smoked could only do so in certain areas, which did not include the bathroom. The teacher took the girls to the vice principal, Theodore Choplick, who was in charge of discipline. Choplick asked each of the girls if she had been smoking in the bathroom.

The first girl immediately admitted that she had, and Choplick gave her a three-day suspension. However, the second girl, who is known to us only as "T.L.O," not only did not admit to smoking in the bathroom, she also denied having been smoking at all. The stage was being set for a confrontation that would eventually reach the Supreme Court.

Choplick then asked for T.L.O's purse so that he might search it. This was something he had commonly done as part of his duties at the school. Immediately, he saw some cigarettes in her purse. But that was not all. He saw some cigarette rolling papers, which in his experience meant that the person who had them was using marijuana.

This convinced Choplick to empty out her bag. He found a pipe, a bag containing a substance that smelled like marijuana, and a little book that contained a list of people who owed the girl money.

These factors convinced Choplick that the girl had been selling marijuana. He called her parents, and then the police, who arrived and explained the Miranda rights to her. Under the questioning of the police, the girl admitted to selling marijuana, and Choplick gave her ten days suspension.

However, the local prosecutor then charged T.L.O with delinquency in juvenile court. Her lawyer fought the juvenile complaint and went to civil court to fight the school suspension, both times using the same argument: Her Fourth Amendment rights had been violated by the vice principal. Therefore, under the exclusionary rule, the evidence against her had to be tossed out.

Up to this point, in the absence of a Supreme Court ruling, three separate theories had evolved about the extent to which school officials were restricted by the Fourth Amendment. The first theory was that the officials were acting in loco parentis, a Latin expression meaning "in the place of the parents." In that case, school officials need not be more restrained in searching a student than a parent would.

Others had argued that the full force of the Fourth Amendment should apply to school officials. Under this theory, they would need to have probable cause and a warrant in order to search a student.

The middle position held that while the Fourth Amendment did indeed protect students, the standards should probably be lower than they would be for adults. While this sounded reasonable, some were troubled by the idea that the schoolchildren would have less protection than people accused of a crime have under the law.

The *T.L.O* case moved slowly through the New Jersey court system, finally reaching the state Supreme Court, which ruled for the moderate position: the Fourth Amendment did indeed apply, but searches only needed to be reasonable, and did not necessarily need a warrant. However, Choplick's search had not been reasonable. He had had no information indicating the purse contained cigarettes. Possession of cigarettes was not even an offense; and merely possessing cigarettes did not mean that the girl had smoked them in a prohibited place. And finally, emptying out the purse on his desk had not been reasonable in any case. Therefore, they suppressed the evidence.

The state of New Jersey immediately appealed to the U.S. Supreme Court, but, interestingly enough, only on the grounds that the exclusionary rule should not apply to searches conducted by school officials, apparently willing to accept the other restrictions imposed by the state court. The U.S. Supreme Court began to hear arguments on the case in 1984, but soon asked each side to expand their arguments beyond the narrow matter of the exclusionary rule to explore precisely what role the Fourth Amendment had in the public school system.

Under those circumstances, it should have come as no surprise that in the end the Court did not rule about the applicability of the exclusionary rule. Instead, it answered, although this time with much greater finality, the issues the New Jersey court had decided. First, the Court said, the Fourth Amendment did indeed apply to the public school system. However, this did not mean that school officials were expected to learn the ins and outs of probable cause to the same degree required of a police officer. Instead, they would be held to a more general standard of whether or not a search was "reasonable under the circumstances." This meant that the search must be made in the expectation that it would turn up evidence that the student had violated the school's rules, and also that the search was not unnecessarily intrusive, given the nature of the suspected violation and the student's age.

The Court then decided that under this standard, Choplick's search had indeed been reasonable in its first goal, finding cigarettes that would tend to disprove her claim that she had not been smoking. Once the rolling papers were found, Choplick was then justified in expanding his search. The entire search from beginning to end had been reasonable, and thus there was no need to consider whether or not the exclusionary rule would apply.

By this point, ironically, T.L.O had already graduated high school and was trying to put the historic events of her freshman year in high school behind her.

Vernonia v. Acton

Ten years later, the Court again addressed the question of whether a student's rights were more limited than those of an adult.

The Vernonia, Oregon school district experienced a rising drug and alcohol problem in the late 1980s. Many of the school district's athletes were the worst offenders, and because of their popularity other students were imitating them and abusing drugs or alcohol as well. The school district began a program of testing all the children in their athletics program for drugs.

The plan called for students who signed up for teams to take a drug test. Then, each week during the season, ten percent of the athletes on the team, chosen randomly, had to take another drug test. The tests were closely monitored to make sure that the students did not try to "cheat" on them. The results were known only to the district superintendent, and if a student failed, he or she was retested. If the second test failed, the student would be sent to drug counseling, or suspended for two seasons.

When a twelve-year-old boy named James Acton decided to try out for the football team, he refused to take the drug test. The school would not let him play without one, though, and Acton's parents sued the school district, claiming that the "blanket" testing violated his Fourth Amendment rights. The case was eventually appealed to the Supreme Court, which issued its decision in 1995.

Acton's basic argument was that the school had no reason to believe that he was taking drugs, and therefore mandatory testing was unreasonable. The majority of the Court disagreed, however. While a child certainly had an "expectation of privacy," it noted, this expectation was less than what an adult enjoyed. Furthermore, athletes, who used a communal locker room where they changed clothes and showered together, had an even lower standard of privacy. In the face of the compelling crisis of drug use in the school district, the school district's right to ensure the safety and health of the majority of its members overrode the privacy concerns of individual students. In a sharp dissent, however, Justice Sandra Day O'Connor noted that she could think of no better summary of the Fourth Amendment's protections than James Acton's basic defense—there was no reason to suspect him of anything.

9 The Fourth Amendment and Searches of Cars

When the Fourth Amendment was written, the primary means of transportation were riding a horse or a horse-drawn wagon, or sailing by ship. However, in the early twentieth century a new form of transportation became overwhelmingly common—the automobile.

Cars present an interesting challenge to interpretations of the Fourth Amendment. On the one hand, they are hardly either the "person" or "house" of a citizen, so they do not seem to be covered by the Fourth Amendment. However, it is undeniable that many people view their cars as part of their personal space, much like their homes. Since 1925, the Supreme Court has had to weigh both these concerns carefully in defining the degree to which the Fourth Amendment protects a person's automobile.

The first case to really address the issues involved in warrantless searches of automobiles was *Carroll v. United States* (1925), decided during Prohibition, when the federal government enforced the Eighteenth Amendment's ban on manufacturing, selling, or transporting alcoholic beverages. George Carroll had been arrested and convicted of transporting liquor on the basis of evidence that had been taken from his car, without a search warrant, by federal agents.

The Court's decision provided the basic framework for all subsequent decisions. Since the Fourth Amendment had been ratified, the Court noted, a fundamental difference had been recognized between a search of a building or other structure, and the search of a wagon or a boat. Simply put, in the latter case there was a very real danger that the evidence would be moved out of the jurisdiction of the officers during the time it took to get a search warrant. The public's interest in obtaining evidence of criminal activity outweighed any expectation of privacy in this case.

By 1949, the precise breadth of this exception to the Fourth Amendment warrant requirement had been spelled out. The police were allowed to search a parked car, because a suspect might move it without their knowledge, for example. The basic rule, which remains in place, is that the police have the right to make a warrantless search whenever they have probable cause that the car has been involved in an illegal activity. Without probable cause, however, the search would be considered unreasonable and the Court has repeatedly thrown out evidence stemming from such searches.

Automobile Searches Since *Mapp v. Ohio*

Since *Mapp v. Ohio* "incorporated" the Fourth Amendment, the Supreme Court's decisions have amounted to a national evidence policy, affecting not only federal agents but state and city police as well. The Court has remained true to the ruling of *Carroll v. United States*, and has allowed police broad exceptions to the warrant requirement when searching cars.

For example, the Court has allowed the police to take paint samples from a car parked in a public parking lot. It has also not required that the police obtain a warrant to search a car that they have impounded, even up to a week later.

However, a series of rulings in the 1970s and early 1980s created a confusing system of exceptions to the warrant requirement that were sometimes apparently contradictory to each other. The Court has with some difficulty tried to straighten out these concerns to make a consistent policy.

Passengers and Searches

A 1978 case addressed the Fourth Amendment concerns of passengers in a car that the police decided to search. In *Rakas v. Illinois*, the Court had to decide if evidence uncovered by the police during a warrantless search of a car could be used against people who were only riding in the car.

The Court decided that it could. The search itself had been reasonable and proper: the police had probable cause, because the car matched the description of a car used as the getaway vehicle in a robbery that had taken place in the area. Furthermore, the Fourth Amendment only protected unreasonable searches of a person's body or property. If the evidence being used against them was found on another person's "premises or property," their Fourth Amendment rights had not been violated. Since none of the passengers claimed to own either the car or the items that were seized by the police, the Fourth Amendment did not apply.

The decision in this case was made by only a 5–4 vote and was sharply criticized by the dissenting justices for making property rights more important than privacy rights.

"Open Season" on Automobile Searches

The minority's concern in *Rakas v. Illinois* was that, as Justice Byron White put it, "open season" would be declared for all searches of automobiles. However, this seemed to be disproved by two further rulings.

The first came only four months after *Rakas*. In *Delaware v. Prouse*, the Court voted 8–1 to find that the police practice of randomly stopping motorists to check their licenses and registrations violated the Fourth Amendment because it did not meet the probable cause test. In the case, William Prouse had been stopped by a Delaware patrolman, but only to check his license and registration; he had not broken any traffic laws. When the patrolman approached his car, however, he smelled marijuana smoke, and looking in saw marijuana lying in plain view on the floor of the car. Prouse was arrested, but during a trial hearing asked for the evidence seized to be suppressed under his Fourth Amendment rights. The case eventually reached the Supreme Court, which agreed with Prouse. Any searches and seizures conducted during a random stoppage without probable cause of a specific crime could not be admitted as evidence. This case also involved issues of the "plain view" (see chapter 5) exceptions, which require the officer to be conducting a legal search—which was not the case here.

Then, in 1981, the Court restricted automobile searches even further. Their ruling in the case of *Robbins v. California* found that in order to search a closed container within a car, such as a piece of luggage, the police must get a warrant, even if their search was otherwise reasonable. This protection, however, was to be short-lived.

United States v. Ross

District of Columbia police had been given a tip from an informant that illegal drugs were being sold from a parked car. Although the police were told the location of the car, when they arrived on the scene they did not see anybody in the area and left. Shortly thereafter they returned to see the car being driven off. They followed the car after noticing that the person driving it matched the description they had been given of the person suspected of selling illegal drugs. They stopped the car and found a pistol inside the glove compartment. One officer then opened the trunk of the car, and found a closed paper bag that, when he opened it, was found to contain heroin. The police arrested the man, Albert Ross, and impounded the car. A search done while the car was impounded also turned up a closed leather pouch that contained a few thousand dollars.

On the basis of this evidence, Ross was convicted. The U.S. Court of Appeals, however, reversed the conviction under the *Robbins* decision, and the United States government (the case took place in the District of Columbia, which is governed directly by the federal government) appealed the case to the Supreme Court.

The Court not only reinstated Ross' conviction but also disposed of the rationale of the *Robbins* case. The limiting factor of any reasonable search, whether conducted with or without a warrant, was not the containers within which evidence was concealed, but probable cause. If there was probable cause to believe that the trunk of a car—as there seemed to be in this case—contained evidence of a crime, the police were justified in searching the trunk and any containers inside it. The Court decided this because the police would have been justified in searching, with a warrant, inside of jars if a place was suspected of being a drug lab. There was no fundamental difference between the scope of a warrantless search and one conducted with a warrant, provided that each one was reasonable. And, since the Court judged that the search in this case was reasonable, the evidence uncovered by the police was admissible.

Decisions Since *United States v. Ross*

Since the *Ross* case, the Court has generally expanded the police's ability to make warrantless searches of automobiles.

In 1991, the case of *California v. Acevedo*, for example, ruled that the police were authorized to search an entire car without a warrant including all closed containers inside it, even if they only had probable cause to think that just one of the containers held evidence.

Michigan v. Sitz, concluded in 1990, found that the police had a right to set up checkpoints to see if people were driving while drunk and to randomly search cars at those checkpoints. The judgment of the court was that the inconvenience that the checkpoints created was only slight, but they did much to discourage drunk driving.

In 1985, the Court ruled that a mobile home still fell under the exceptions given to regular cars. In *California v. Carney*, the police had searched, without a warrant, the mobile home of a person suspected of giving boys marijuana for sex, and discovered evidence of drug use that was used to convict the owner of the mobile home. The Court upheld the reasonableness of their search, because the mobile home was fully capable of being driven and was located in a public space, a parking lot in downtown San Diego. However, the Court took pains to note that both these qualifications had to be present in order for a mobile home to be considered an automobile, and not a home deserving the protection of the Fourth Amendment.

In 1996, the Court ruled that even if the police have another crime in mind, they are authorized to stop a car that has violated a traffic law and search it without a warrant. The case, *Whren v. United States*, involved two black men who had been pulled over on a minor traffic complaint and searched. They were found to have crack cocaine with them. They argued, however, that the police were then following people they suspected of committing more serious crimes until they violated a traffic law—in violation of the probable cause limitation of the Fourth Amendment. But the Court rejected this because it claimed that the police had the right to pull over and search people who broke the traffic laws, even if the police had "bigger game" on their minds. This thinking has been criticized in light of the controversial allegations of racial profiling, the practice of pulling over people of color more often than white people.

This chapter has dealt with the consequences of one new technology the founders could hardly have anticipated: the automobile. The next chapter explores the world of electronic communication and surveillance, other forms of technology that have raised many issues involving the protections of the Fourth Amendment.

10 Electronic Surveillance and the Fourth Amendment

When the Fourth Amendment was ratified, the primary means of communication over distance in the United States was the written letter, which was clearly protected as a person's "papers." Such future inventions as the telegraph, telephone, and radio were obviously beyond the ability of the founders to predict. At the start of the twentieth century, however, these technologies were so prevalent that constitutional questions about them finally had to be resolved by the Supreme Court.

The court has been faced with two basic kinds of electronic surveillance: wiretapping, the use of equipment to listen in on private telephone calls, and the use of electronic "bugs" to listen in on private conversations. Both kinds of surveillance are the same in that the people who are being overheard do not know that they are being monitored.

The first Supreme Court case involving electronic surveillance of any kind was the 1928 case of *Olmstead v. United States*. This controversial 5–4 decision caused severe disagreement within the Court itself.

The case involved the use of wiretaps by federal agents to gather evidence about a bootlegging ring. This evidence was used to convict the members of the ring, who had appealed, claiming that the agents had violated their Fourth Amendment rights. Chief justice (and former president) William Howard Taft disagreed. The Fourth Amendment, he claimed, only protected physical things, such as papers or contraband. The agents, by merely listening in on conversations, had neither performed a search nor seized any evidence. Therefore, Fourth Amendment protections did not apply, but Congress could pass laws forbidding the use of wiretaps.

Both Justice Oliver Wendell Holmes Jr. and Justice Louis Brandeis dissented vigorously. Both noted that wiretapping was already illegal under federal law for private individuals to perform; surely the government should not be allowed to commit a crime, even if it was to convict a criminal. Justice Brandeis further argued that science and technology were continuing to advance, and that future innovations might be able to accomplish far greater invasions of privacy than merely listening in on phone conversations. Yet under this decision, the Fourth Amendment would not protect people from such invasions; without the protection of that amendment, the government would not even need a warrant to listen in on any citizen, regardless of whether or not they were suspected of committing a crime.

Congress took to heart Chief Justice Taft's suggestion to pass legislation prohibiting wiretapping by federal agents. In 1934, Congress passed the Federal Communications Act, which prohibited anyone not "authorized" by the sender of a communication from revealing its meaning or existence, which boiled down to a strict prohibition against using information gathered by eavesdropping. The Court handed down this interpretation in *Nardone v. United States* (1937), which found that federal agents, and any other persons, were forbidden to use wiretaps to intercept telephone calls. By 1939, the Court had forbidden the use of any evidence obtained either directly or indirectly from wiretaps.

During World War II, when (rightly or wrongly) issues of national security took precedence in the minds of many, the Court retreated somewhat from the position of forbidding all evidence derived from wiretaps. In the cases of *Goldstein v. United States* and *Goldman v. United States*, both decided in 1942, the Court allowed the use of some evidence acquired by electronic surveillance. In the *Goldstein* case, the Court allowed the use of evidence derived from wiretapped conversations provided it was about a person who was not a part of the telephone conversation. And in *Goldman*, the Court decided that evidence obtained from a hidden electronic bug did not violate the Federal Communications Act. The Court still operated under the *Olmstead* ruling, and so the Fourth Amendment could not be considered in this decision.

In *Silverman v. United States* (1961), however, the Court disallowed evidence that had been collected with an electronic bug. The important factor in this case was that the bug had been physically driven into a wall. This was judged to be intrusive by the Court, and set the stage for the much more dramatic decision in *Katz v. United States*.

Katz v. United States

Charles Katz had been indicted in federal court for eight counts of operating an illegal bookmaking ring. The evidence against

The Supreme Court has generally favored restricting government or law enforcement's use of wiretaps or other forms of electronic surveillance.

him had been gathered in a creative fashion: instead of bugging his office or tapping his phone, the federal agents had placed a listening device on the outside of a public telephone booth that Katz often used. This allowed them to eavesdrop on Katz's conversations. Because the bug was in a public location, and because it did not penetrate the wall of the booth, under previous rulings it would seem that the use of evidence obtained with it would be legal under the Fourth Amendment.

When the Court heard Katz's appeal in 1967, however, it disagreed. By closing the door to the phone booth, Katz had created a space where he had every expectation of privacy. This was the crucial issue, not whether or not the bug actually penetrated the wall of the booth.

The Court then discredited the idea that electronic eavesdropping did not constitute a search. Declaring that the Fourth Amendment only protected property, not privacy, had been discredited, so the Court ruled that such eavesdropping was in fact a constitutional search. As such, it fell under the guidelines of the Fourth Amendment, including the need to obtain a warrant from a neutral magistrate after demonstrating probable cause and the exclusionary rule.

In 1969, the Court further ruled that defendants whose Fourth Amendment rights had been violated by electronic surveillance had to be presented with all the information collected against them. They could then challenge the parts of the evidence that the government was going to use to prosecute them. In many cases this resulted in the government dropping charges against them, out of concern that handing over this information would reveal too much information on the methods the government had used to eavesdrop.

Congress had by that time passed the 1968 Crime Control and Safe Streets Act. This law tried to create guidelines for government officials that would match the *Katz* ruling. In order for agents to begin electronic surveillance, they first had to get the approval of the Justice Department, and then a warrant from a federal judge.

This act came into question in 1972, when the Court was asked to decide whether or not the president's actions could be exempted from normal Fourth Amendment standards. In *United States v. United States District Court*, the Court was asked to judge whether or not a warrantless wiretapping ordered by President Nixon could be considered legal.

The case involved a man named Plamondon, who was accused of having attempted to blow up the Central Intelligence Agency's office in Ann Arbor, Michigan. He moved to have the government disclose whether or not it had used wiretapping to gather evidence against him. The government admitted that it had done so, without a warrant, but claimed that the Crime Control Act of 1969 permitted the president to order such a wiretap when national security demanded it. A district court disagreed, and the government asked the Supreme Court to reverse the decision.

The Court did not do so. While noting that there were indeed some exceptions to the requirement that the government obtain a warrant before conducting a search, there were only a few of these and they generally existed to protect the life of law enforcement officers. Nor did the language of the Act support the government's claim. The Act only noted that it did not restrict the president's existing powers; the Court found that these did not include the ability to order a warrantless search, even when issues of national security were involved. The Court had faith that the judges who were asked to grant warrants in these cases would take the national security issues into consideration when deciding whether or not to grant the warrant. The Court therefore reaffirmed the decision of the district court.

This was not the only time the Court ruled against the Nixon administration in a wiretapping case. In 1974, the Court decided against the administration in *United States v. Giordano*. This case involved authorizations for wiretapping issued by the government but signed not by Attorney General John N. Mitchell or his deputy, but by an aide, in violation of the Crime Control Act of 1969, which required the attorney general's signature on such authorizations. Hundreds of warrants were thus invalidated, and the evidence collected by their wiretapping had to be thrown out.

In the last few chapters, we have explored specific areas the Supreme Court has ruled upon. The next chapter will examine a few other areas of interest that the Court has ruled upon that do not quite fit into the broad categories previously examined.

11 Other Fourth Amendment Areas

This chapter will investigate some of the lesser-known areas of Fourth Amendment rights, such as searches at international borders and in open fields.

Border Searches

In general, the Court has found that the Fourth Amendment protections apply to searches of cars conducted near the border. It has, however, found certain important exceptions.

The first major case in this area was the 1973 decision in *Almeida-Sanchez v. United States*. The defendant in this case had been stopped while driving on a highway in California some twenty miles from the border, by a unit of the United States Border Patrol. The Border Patrol had been authorized by federal law to look for illegal aliens anywhere within one hundred miles of the U.S. border.

Acting without a search warrant, the agents searched the defendant's car and found marijuana in it. He was arrested and convicted of illegally transporting marijuana across the border. His appeal ended up in the Supreme Court, which reversed his conviction. Although the government clearly had the right to exclude aliens from the country, and this right included searches at the border, or where a "functional" border might exist—for example, by searching passengers and luggage from an international flight that went directly to Chicago at O'Hare airport—the Court ruled that searching Almeida-Sanchez's car twenty miles from the border was wholly unreasonable.

Two years later, the Court's ruling in *United States v. Ortiz* went even further. The Court found that searches conducted at an official checkpoint that was sixty-six miles from the border, at the discretion of the officers and without probable cause, were also unreasonable. A separate ruling in *United States v. Brignoni-Ponce*, issued that same day, said that probable cause did not include the fact that the occupants of a car "appeared to be" Mexican. However, the Court specifically left open the matter of stopping a car merely to question its occupants. Also, the *Brignoni-Ponce* decision stated that the full standard of probable cause did not need to be fulfilled when the Border Patrol stopped people to question them as to whether or not they were aliens.

In 1976, the Court found that non-intrusive visual searches of cars conducted at a border checkpoint did not violate the Fourth Amendment. The case, *United States v. Martinez-Fuerte* involved the practice of slowing traffic down at the border checkpoint and then sending cars the Border Patrol had picked out to a separate area, where their occupants were questioned. Since the intrusion was much less than the searches conducted in the other rulings, they did not violate Fourth Amendment standards.

Open Fields

The law has long recognized that a person's "home" can entail more than just the physical building he or she lives in. For example, a person's porch or even his or her backyard is certainly not only part of the grounds where he or she lives, but can be considered part of the "home" for Fourth Amendment purposes. In other words, before the area can be searched, the government must acquire a search warrant. These outlying areas are known in legal terms as the "curtilage." In 1984, the Court was asked to rule how far the curtilage extended in *Oliver v. United States*.

Kentucky State Police agents had received a tip that marijuana was being grown on Craig Oliver's farm. They went to the farm and found a footpath leading beyond a locked gate that had a "No Trespassing" sign on it; at the end of the path, nearly a mile from Oliver's house, was a field of marijuana. Oliver was arrested, but before the trial began he moved that the "evidence" of the field's existence be suppressed. The case eventually was appealed to the Supreme Court.

In 1924, in *Hester v. United States*, the Court had ruled that open fields, such as pastures and vacant lots, were not protected by the Fourth Amendment. They upheld this doctrine in the *Oliver* case as well. Although in this case the field was remote and well hidden from the public view, the issue was not whether or not the area was "private," but rather whether the government's action violated the "personal and societal values protected by the Fourth Amendment." In this case, they did not. The field was too far removed from Oliver's house to be considered part of his curtilage, and the evidence was allowed to stand.

William H. Rehnquist

William H. Rehnquist (born 1924) is the current chief justice of the Supreme Court. He was appointed to the Supreme Court in 1971 as an associate justice, then appointed by Ronald Reagan in 1986 to replace the retiring Warren Burger. As a young man, he was a noted conservative lawyer and became an assistant attorney general in the Nixon Administration.

More conservative than his predecessor, Rehnquist has been on the majority in many cases that restricted the liberal decisions of the Warren Court. In 1999, Rehnquist entered history as only the second chief justice to preside over the trial in the Senate of an impeached president, William Jefferson Clinton, who was acquitted.

Since the *Oliver* ruling, the Court has allowed further warrantless searches even within the curtilage of a home. In *California v. Ciraolo* (1986), it ruled that the way in which the police obtained the evidence that the defendant was growing marijuana in his backyard was admissible. The ruling was based on the fact that the police, by flying over the man's backyard, had only observed what anyone flying across the land could have observed; therefore, there could not be a reasonable expectation of privacy. Further rulings have upheld this doctrine, even when the police use special cameras capable of taking pictures at a distance where the details would not be visible to the naked eye. The open fields doctrine has also justified police searches of garbage that has been left out in the street for collection, under the idea that there can be no reasonable expectation of privacy for discarded materials left in public view.

Personal Searches: What Constitutes a Search?

The Court has ruled at various times about searches of a person's clothing, as in *Terry v. Ohio* (see chapter 8). However, what protection does a person have against searches of his or her body? And what about fingerprints or blood samples? Does collecting samples of either of these constitute a search?

The basic principle in these cases was set out by Justice Oliver Wendell Holmes in the 1910 case of *Holt v. United States*. In his decision, Holmes ruled that a person's body need not be excluded as evidence under the Fourth Amendment. Furthermore, characteristics of a public nature can be "seized" by the government and used as evidence without violating the Fifth Amendment's protection against self-incrimination.

This doctrine has been used to allow the collection of voice samples, without a warrant, to identify a suspect. It similarly allows the use of handwriting samples; since a person's handwriting is knowingly exposed to the public every day, no expectation of privacy exists. Likewise, fingerprints, which are left on every physical object we touch, are allowed to be collected by the government without a warrant.

However, the Court has ruled that collecting evidence from certain bodily traits is intrusive enough to be considered a search under the Fourth Amendment. For example, while a person's fingerprints are a kind of "public statement" not protected by the Fourth Amendment, scraping under a person's fingernails to find evidence of a crime is considered a search and requires a warrant. Since 1966, the Court has also considered blood tests to be searches. Under this logic,

A person's fingerprints can be used as evidence in the courts since no expectation of privacy exists in leaving them.

the Court refused to allow the state of Virginia to remove a bullet from the chest of a man who might have been wounded during a robbery. Although the bullet might prove that he was guilty, the Court found that drugging a citizen not yet convicted of a crime, and performing surgery on him was too severe an invasion of privacy to be allowed.

Drug testing has also raised Fourth Amendment issues. Both the taking of urine samples and breath testing have been deemed searches by the Court. Breath tests require that air be expelled from deep within the lungs, which was close enough to a blood test in the Court's eyes. And while urine tests would seem to only involve material that has left the body, the fact that chemical analysis of it could reveal many facts about a person made it invasive enough, in the Court's eyes, to qualify it as a search.

Conclusion

The Fourth Amendment to the Constitution has, in the end, been one of the greatest guarantees of liberty in our country's history. This little amendment, with its somewhat ambiguous wording, has over time expanded its ability to protect people's rights.

Even before the Revolutionary War, Americans believed that a limited government was the best protection they could have for their liberty. Indeed, the Revolution itself was caused in large measure by attempts on the part of the British government to exert more direct power over the colonists.

Americans have also been suspicious of attempts by the government to intrude upon their privacy and personal space. In a very real sense, liberty, especially American liberty, is the freedom to be "let alone," to not be interfered with by the government.

This basic philosophy is reflected at every level of our Constitution. No other government has a basic document that contains so many rules on what a government may not do. While the federal government is given large and important powers under the Constitution, these are constantly restricted by the language of the document, and checked by the structure of the government itself, which was carefully designed so that each branch balances out the others.

Yet even this was not enough for the generation that fought the Revolution. They demanded further assurances that the government would not infringe upon their daily lives. They feared a powerful central government that could take away the liberty that had cost them so much to achieve.

So, in an act of political courage and commitment, James Madison, who had opposed the idea when he was the principal architect of the Constitution, helped create the Bill of Rights. These ten amendments are filled with "shall not" and "must not." They further limit the government's power, and set out starkly what the rights of a free citizen are to be in the United States. Indeed, the only mention of granting powers and rights comes in the Tenth Amendment, which concludes that all rights not mentioned so far are to be held by the people.

Yet this promise of liberty was slow in coming for many people in the United States. Even after the bloody disaster of the Civil War, which forever changed the influence of the federal government on the lives of Americans, many citizens still found that because of prejudice, they were denied the harvest of freedom that the Bill of Rights had sown.

This was especially true in matters relating to criminal trials. For many years, the full protection guaranteed by the Bill of Rights was unavailable to many, because the Bill of Rights itself did not apply to the states.

A democracy's greatest test may well be its criminal trials. Nowhere else does the fine balance that must be struck between public and private rights become so clear, so critical, and so crucial. For here is the most powerful test of the basic ideal of American freedom: that no man, in the eyes of the law, is better or worse than another. At the same time, the criminal justice system is a test of whether or not the government's interests are ever to be placed above those of a citizen who is only accused of a crime, and who has yet to be proven guilty.

The founders had long experience with injustice during the colonial days. They knew that the British general warrants had been terrible tools of oppression, used to ruthlessly attack those who opposed the government, as well as to terrify and cow citizens into complying with unjust laws. Thus, one of the fundamental protections placed into the Bill of Rights was a freedom from these unreasonable searches and seizures.

At the same time, the government must be allowed some ability to look for and acquire evidence of a crime. Society has a terribly important interest in punishing criminals, for if allowing the government too much power can create an injustice by convicting innocent men, just as terrible an injustice occurs when the guilty are allowed to go free. Thus, while the basic concept of the Fourth Amendment is not controversial, almost any application of it is bound for debate, for it is here that we find the most powerful collision between the interests of the state and the interests of a citizen.

In its rulings on the Fourth Amendment, the Court has charted the changing vision of American liberty. At first it was seen as a protection of property rights, the property rights that were so dear to the founders and were another major cause of the Revolution. Yet, just as the vision of the Bill of Rights has been expanded over time from merely a description of what the federal government will not do against an individual to a positive assertion of the basic freedoms possessed by everyone in the United States that cannot be breached by any government, so has the Fourth Amendment's interpretation changed. A new right, the right to privacy, has grown out of it, and intrusions into a person's privacy, not seizures of his property, are now seen as its main protection.

This leads to its implementation at a trial. Over the years, the Court has continued to expand the Fourth Amendment's protections, adopting the doctrine of the exclusionary rule to make inadmissible any evidence seized in violation of the Amendment's protections. This controversial rule, as noted previously, is almost unique to American justice; yet such is the standard of liberty demanded by the Constitution, or so the members of the Supreme Court have decided.

Likewise, deciding exactly when the public interest demands that the Fourth Amendment's protections be overridden has caused no end of controversy. Each time, the Court has had to weigh the question of the greater injustice: allowing someone who may be guilty to go free, or restricting the liberty of other people in similar circumstances. It is no wonder, then, that so many times Fourth Amendment rulings have been reversed by later Courts who found that the previous standards did not fit with more recent conceptions of liberty.

In this book, you have read about many Supreme Court decisions. Some may have surprised you. Some you may agree with; others you may strongly disagree with. Yet this process, as imperfect as it may seem, has kept the Constitution and the Bill of Rights living, breathing documents that continue to define not only what it is to be an American, but what it is to be free.

Preamble to the Constitution

We the People of the United States, in order to form a more perfect Union, establish Justice, insure domestic Tranquility, provide for the common defence, promote the general Welfare, and secure the Blessings of Liberty to ourselves and our Posterity, do ordain and establish this Constitution for the United States of America.

On September 25, 1789, Congress transmitted to the state legislatures twelve proposed amendments, two of which, having to do with congressional representation and congressional pay, were not adopted. The remaining ten amendments became the Bill of Rights.

The Bill of Rights

Amendment I

Congress shall make no law respecting an establishment of religion, or prohibiting the free exercise thereof; or abridging the freedom of speech, or of the press; or the right of the people peaceably to assemble, and to petition the Government for a redress of grievances.

Amendment II

A well regulated Militia, being necessary to the security of a free State, the right of the people to keep and bear Arms, shall not be infringed.

Amendment III

No Soldier shall, in time of peace be quartered in any house, without the consent of the Owner, nor in time of war, but in a manner to be prescribed by law.

Amendment IV

The right of the people to be secure in their persons, houses, papers, and effects, against unreasonable searches and seizures, shall not be violated, and no Warrants shall issue, but upon probable cause, supported by Oath or affirmation, and particularly describing the place to be searched, and the persons or things to be seized.

Amendment V

No person shall be held to answer for a capital, or otherwise infamous crime, unless on a presentment or indictment of a Grand Jury, except in cases arising in the land or naval forces, or in the Militia, when in actual service in time of War or public danger; nor shall any person be subject for the same offence to be twice put in jeopardy of life or limb; nor shall be compelled in any criminal case to be a witness against himself, nor be deprived of life, liberty, or property, without due process of law; nor shall private property be taken for public use, without just compensation.

Amendment VI

In all criminal prosecutions, the accused shall enjoy the right to a speedy and public trial, by an impartial jury of the State and district wherein the crime shall have been committed, which district shall have been previously ascertained by law, and to be informed of the nature and cause of the accusation; to be confronted with the witnesses against him; to have compulsory process for obtaining witnesses in his favor, and to have the Assistance of Counsel for his defence.

Amendment VII

In Suits at common law, where the value in controversy shall exceed twenty dollars, the right of trial by jury shall be preserved, and no fact tried by a jury, shall be otherwise re-examined in any Court of the United States, than according to the rules of the common law.

Amendment VIII

Excessive bail shall not be required, nor excessive fines imposed, nor cruel and unusual punishments inflicted.

Amendment IX

The enumeration in the Constitution, of certain rights, shall not be construed to deny or disparage others retained by the people.

Amendment X

The powers not delegated to the United States by the Constitution, nor prohibited by it to the States, are reserved to the States respectively, or to the people.

Glossary

appeal Asking a higher court to review the decision in a case and change it.

attainder, bill of A law that declares a person guilty of a crime without giving him or her a trial, and imposes a sentence. Specifically forbidden in the United States by the Constitution.

certiorari, writ of Special order issued by the Supreme Court granting an opportunity to appeal to it.

checks and balances Fundamental principle behind the construction of the U.S. government. Each branch of government has certain powers granted to it, but each branch has the power to prevent the other branches from abusing their powers.

conviction Decision by a jury (or judge) that a person is guilty of a crime they have been charged with.

counsel A lawyer who assists a person with their defense.

defendant In criminal cases, the person who has been indicted for a crime.

evidence Any information that relates to whether or not a person has committed a crime. Evidence may be physical, such as blood samples, or consist of the testimony of witnesses, and the opinion of experts about other evidence in the trial.

ex post facto Latin for "after the fact." In constitutional studies, writing a law that punishes a person for an action that was not a crime at the time the action was taken; forbidden by the Constitution.

jurisdiction The power of a court to hear a specific case. Courts are limited to the kinds of cases they can hear by the laws of their government.

overturn To change the decision of a lower court, or a precedent.

probable cause Reasonable belief, based on the evidence presented, that a person has committed a crime; necessary in order to obtain a warrant or indictment.

reverse To change the ruling of a lower court or a precedent to an opposite direction.

suspect A person believed to have committed a crime, but who has not yet been indicted.

testimony Statements of a witness during a trial.

warrant Document, issued by a judge or other magistrate, authorizing the arrest of a person, or the search of a specific area for evidence of a crime; the warrant must include a specific charge or charges, and probable cause that the person has committed the crime must be shown to the magistrate.

For More Information

Electronic Frontier Foundation
1550 Bryant Street, Suite 725
San Francisco, CA 94103-4832
(415) 436-9333
http://www.eff.org

National Institute of Justice
633 Indiana Avenue NW
Washington, DC 20531
(202) 307-2942
http://www.ojp.usdoj.gov/nij

Supreme Court of the United States
1 First Street NE
Washington, DC 20543
(202) 479-3211
http://www.supremecourtus.gov

United States Department of Justice
P.O. Box 65808

Washington, DC 20035-5808
(202) 514-2151
http://www.usdoj.gov/crt/crt-home.html

Web Sites

http://www.law.cornell.edu
Cornell Law School's Web site provides Supreme Court decisions since 1990 and cases of historic interest.

http://oyez.at.nwu.edu/oyez.html
Northwestern University provides this service, which has recordings of oral arguments before the Supreme Court.

http://www.law.emory.edu
This site from the Emory University School of Law includes a searchable U.S. Constitution and links to other law sites and the various branches of government

http://www.yale.edu/lawweb/avalon/avalon.htm
This Yale University site contains important documents from U.S. history, including the Constitution, the Articles of Confederation, treaties, and letters.

http://www.nara.gov/
This National Archives site is home to the Constitution, searchable databases of presidential papers, the U.S. Code, and many other features.

For Further Reading

Abernathy, M. Glenn, and Barbara A. Perry. *Civil Liberties Under the Constitution*. Columbia, SC: University of South Carolina Press, 1993.

Alderman, Ellen, and Caroline Kennedy. *In Our Defense: The Bill of Rights in Action*. New York, Morrow, 1991.

Alderman, Ellen, and Caroline Kennedy. *The Right to Privacy*. New York: Knopf, 1995.

Amar, Akhil Reed. *The Bill of Rights: Creation and Reconstruction*. New Haven, CT: Yale University Press, 1998.

Biskupic, Joan, and Elder Witt. *The Supreme Court and Individual Rights*. Washington, DC: Congressional Quarterly, Inc., 1997

Hickok, Edward W., Jr., ed. *The Bill of Rights: Original Meaning and Current Understanding*. Charlottesville, NC: University of Virginia Press, 1991.

Lieberman, Jethro K. *A Practical Companion to the Constitution*. Berkeley, CA: University of California Press, 1999.

Index

Photo Credits

Cover image: the Constitution of the United States of America; pp. 13, 15, 17, 21, 23, 30, 39, 49, 65, 89 © Bettmann/Corbis; p. 29 © Hulton Getty Collection/Archive Photos; p. 37 © Bob Rowan: Progressive Image/Corbis; p. 41 © Archive Photos; p. 59 © Ed Kashi/Corbis; p. 67 © Corbis; p. 95 © AFP/Corbis; p. 97 © Stephanie Maze/Corbis.

Series Design and Layout

Danielle Goldblatt